TO
GOVERN
A *Changing*
SOCIETY

TO
GOVERN
A *Changing*
SOCIETY

CONSTITUTIONALISM AND THE CHALLENGE
OF NEW TECHNOLOGY   ROBERT S. PECK, *editor*

Smithsonian Institution Press   Washington and London

Editor: Joanne Reams
Designer: Janice Wheeler
Production Editor: Duke Johns

Library of Congress Cataloging-in-Publication Data
To govern a changing society : constitutionalism and the challenge of
    new technology / edited by Robert S. Peck.   p.   cm.
        ISBN 0-87474-783-X (alk. paper)
            1. Civil rights—Congresses.   2. State, The—Congresses.
        3. Technology—Philosophy—Congresses.   4. Technology—Social
        aspects—Congresses.   I. Peck, Robert S.
        JC571.T57 1990
        306.2—dc20   89-39868
British Library Cataloguing-in-Publication Data available
Manufactured in the United States of America
97 96 95 94 93 92 91 90   5 4 3 2 1

∞The paper used in this publication meets the minimum
requirements of the American National Standard for
Permanence of Paper for Printed Library Materials
z39.48–1984.

CONTENTS

For Valentine —
who likes
the London symposium
on a related
topic .
as ever,
Wilton

ACKNOWLEDGMENTS

The June 4, 1989, Beijing student demonstrations—with the emergence of a "Chinese" Statue of Liberty—nearly coincided with the two-hundredth anniversary of the French Revolution, the Declaration of Rights of Man and Citizen, and the U.S. Bill of Rights. Once again, modern communications technology helped increase world consciousness of fellow humans searching for freedom. As this eclectic collection of essays goes to press, the collapsing Berlin Wall reappears on television screens along with pictures of thousands of East Germans streaming westward; South Africa enters a new phase of weakening *apartheid;* Palestinians agonize; Kafka's Prague loosens after the rippling effects of *glasnost* and *perestroika;* Danielle Mitterrand invites Senator Claiborne Pell and other leaders to Paris for dialogues about the fate of the Kurds; and Gene Roddenberry's *Star Trek: The Next Generation* features an episode about a galactic court case to determine whether Commander Data, an android, has rights.

Such are the outward manifestations of a deep and nearly universal quest: finding a yin-yang balance between the needs for freedom and order. These essays were commissioned for the 1983 Smithsonian celebration of George Orwell's *1984*.

Some have been revised to reflect changing circumstances, but the ideas in all remain true, illustrating the enduring aspects of how humans try to govern themselves in different times, different places, different cultures, and different scales of human organization: the family, the tribe, the farm, the corporation, the nation-state, and trading institutions making up the global economy.

The genesis of the idea for a symposium honoring Orwell can be found in Paul Perrot, a philosophically and morally astute specialist on medieval glass, who now presides over the Richmond Museum of Art. The crafting of much of the original symposium, "The Road after 1984: High Technology and Human Freedom," reflects the historical and anthropological insights of Eliot Dismore Chapple, a pioneer in the study of human interactions, and the wisdom of José Ortega y Gasset. (Chapple set forth the theory that every person has a biological need for freedom of initiative, a partial basis for his proposition that human animals are not driven genetically to cohere in mass herding but prefer working and living in smaller groups.) The much-cited political scientist Lewis Anthony Dexter, a relative of suffragette Susan B. Anthony, wrote extensively on constitutionalism when he read these essays. His "deep background" papers reinforced the knowledge Robert S. Peck brought, as a lawyer, to the writing of his introduction and the editing of the essays.

The Advisory Group for the Office of Smithsonian Symposia and Seminars (now the Office of Interdisciplinary Studies) endorsed the idea of honoring Orwell and further recommended that the political and social implications of technology be explored in the process. Thus an earlier volume of essays, edited by Lewis H. Lapham of *Harper's* magazine (*High Technology and Human Freedom*), contains an essay by Douglas Cater, "Can the Mass Media Control Our Thoughts?" The chairman for the Advisory Group was Robert Multhauf, Smithsonian historian of technology.

I owe a personal debt to S. Dillon Ripley, secretary emeritus of the Smithsonian, for his continuing support of the institution's international symposia as a means of restoring the art of the essay; to Mathilda, the Duchess of Argyll, for arranging for me to look, through her telescope, at the bleak Island of Jura, where Orwell wrote *1984*; to the late Geoffrey Gorer, my anthropologist friend who put his friend Eric Blair (George Orwell) on the train when he left to fight for the anarchists in Spain and who introduced me years later to Lady Orwell; to T. R. Fyvel, author and another Orwell friend, who was the last to see Orwell alive. Mr. Fyvel graciously took on the task of heading the symposium after the death of Dame Rebecca West, who had agreed to that task through the intercessions of Dillon Ripley and Professor Evelyn Hutchinson.

Especially, I wish to thank our generous patrons from the worlds of foundations, corporations, and trade unions who responded to my pleas for help. They produced not only money but also ideas. Their own experience at governance in changing societies became a part of the data and insight revealed through the symposium. The management of the symposium and its academic procession lay in the able hands of my colleagues, the late Dorothy Richardson, Barrick Groom, Carla M. Borden, Helen Leavitt, Jutta Lewis, and Melanie Rock. Valerie Jo Fletcher, a painting and sculpture curator at the Hirshhorn Museum and Sculpture Garden, was responsible for the stunning exhibition, "Dreams and Nightmares: Utopian Visions in Modern Art," assembled to coincide with the symposium. Advanced Micro Devices, Inc., commissioned the symposium poster.

The late Clare Booth Luce is fondly remembered for the unexpected drama she brought to the symposium when she was invited to the stage by Susan Stamberg, moderator for the panel on mass media and thought control.

Above all, thanks to George Orwell for his prophetic fear that collectivism would create societies of rootless individuals in urban squalor, ready for new slogans and new beliefs engineered by Big

Brother. That fear, happily, has not been transformed into a self-fulfilling prophecy. His warning, though still descriptive of some societies, may have helped trigger the remarkable break-up of totalitarian empires under way today and should further serve as a warning to citizens of the ever-present temptation to find authoritarian quick fixes even in societies with long democratic traditions.

Robert Peck sets the stage for understanding these tendencies in his introductory essay on constitutions as collections of a nation's core values and on how technology interacts with these values either to liberate or to restrict liberty. Special thanks to him and this book's thirteen contributors.

Wilton S. Dillon

Chairman, Smithsonian Council for Research
on Contemporary Cultures and Civilizations

INTRODUCTION

ROBERT S. PECK

We in the United States take our liberties for granted. This is a truth easily acknowledged and frequently lamented, yet little is done about it. Perhaps our benign neglect results less from confidence that our civil liberties can survive any challenge than from a collective inability to imagine the circumstances that would place our long-secure freedoms in jeopardy.

It is not difficult to imagine a society where freedom does not exist. Authoritarian regimes and even some democratic republics commit vicious crimes against human rights, as newspaper reports indicate every day. In these societies, national survival has elevated security to a more important status than individual liberty enjoys. The terror without makes the terror within tolerable, or at least that is the theory. The state's inexorable drive for survival leads it to distrust its citizens and to employ tantalizing new technologies to intrude on their privacy in search of sedition.

Still, there is another, equally irresistible drive at work here: a desire for liberty, justice, and equality that no regime can ever extinguish. This pang resounds in the souls of all thinking individuals, who often struggle against long and seemingly insurmountable odds to sustain the hope that is the source of their power.

In the United States, the people place their faith in the Constitution. It will protect us, we casually assume, from enemies who would take those liberties away. To us, and our litigious culture, the Constitution has become the legal equivalent of a "Star Wars" weapon—an armament capable of destroying challenges to our liberties as soon as they are launched. However, our ultimate line of defense against tyranny—our great legal tradition notwithstanding—is not the Constitution, but the culture that engendered it and it, in turn, enriches. Certainly, as Justice Louis D. Brandeis wrote, "the greatest menace to freedom is an inert people." The durability of constitutional principles in the United States has been a result of the activist nature of its people. This vitality, inbred as a part of our culture, provides a valuable lesson to those who study governing charters. Constitutionalism, often described narrowly as government according to constitutional principles, is actually the development, refinement, and maintenance of a governing culture. A constitution is merely words on paper that can be conspiratorially ignored, even by the people as a whole.

All but a handful of the world's 165 countries have constitutions. Many of these constitutions are observed more in the breach than in the practice. It is not surprising that constitutions hold so little sway. They are remote documents, or so they seem much of the time. They constitute; they establish a governmental structure. Though the governors must deal with the process and limitations imposed by a constitution, the governed are generally unconcerned with these technicalities. The public's ennui allows those who govern to do so without substantial scrutiny and thus to search the constitutional limitations for loopholes, which tend to become enlarged over time until the constitution and the government become two wholly different systems, one merely theoretical, the other real.

In the United States, the value of liberty is unassailable, a part of the heritage of every living American, no matter how recent an immigrant. The American creed that exalts liberty above almost all else is a direct result of our own national mythology. We are proud that our nation was born when we overthrew a tyrannical foreign power that was the greatest military force the world had seen. Our revolution had higher goals than mere independence; it was aimed at securing liberty, justice, and equality. Ever since that victory, as remarkable as David's over Goliath, we have striven to realize that cause. Whatever mistakes we have made along the way—and there have been many—have failed to obscure the goal or lead us away from it, even when the progress has not been as steady or as smooth as one would hope.

The Constitution was an attempt to realize those qualities of heart and mind that drove the Revolution. Our great leaders—among them George Washington, who led us to victory, and Thomas Jefferson, who gave vision to our common aspirations—convinced us that we could achieve the good society. Each wave of immigrants settling in our land has accepted that belief and renewed it.

That American ethic has held together the dream of human freedom for this country. Every challenge to it has been blunted and turned into a device to further the American cause. Rather than view the Civil War as a failure of the Constitution and the system it established, we prefer to see it as a triumph for the system and the people, another glorious chapter in freedom's story. The myth as much as the reality, the circumstances and mores as much as the statutes and regulations—these have been the hallmarks of the American constitutional culture.

Our faith in the magically protective qualities of our Constitution has lulled us, though, into believing that having a constitution is enough. The hallowed place we reserve for the Constitution leads us to believe that liberty goes hand in hand with the concept of constitutionalism. We could not be more wrong.

Senator J. William Fulbright correctly observed in 1964: "We are inclined to confuse freedom and democracy, which we regard as moral principles, with the way in which these are practiced in America—with capitalism, federalism, and the two-party system, which are not moral principles, but simply the accepted practices of the American people." Freedom can be observed in many ways— ways that differ markedly from the American system.

It is true as well that constitutionalism can be as oppressive as it can be libertarian. The type of society enshrined in a constitution is shaped by the values of the culture that adopts the document. Constitutions—whether observed or not—often establish individual rights, such as freedom of religion and speech and freedom from governmental intrusions of personal privacy. Whether the freedoms pronounced in a constitution are practiced or discarded, however, is often an element of the prevailing national culture. As Justice Antonin Scalia wryly observed with just a bit of hyperbole, "In dictatorships of the modern world, bills of rights are a dime a dozen." A culture that values individual human dignity will take these rights seriously; one that is more collectivist or community oriented may not.

Societies are frequently called upon to make policy decisions that appear to cost little in terms of liberty in order to achieve great dividends in terms of security. Individually, each of these decisions seems to come out favorably for the security interests that are involved, when put to a cost-benefit analysis. Cumulatively, however, these decisions contain the strong possibility that, imperceptibly, the government will have turned a corner that places it in a category akin to authoritarianism. When this happens little by little, it is virtually impossible to detect the precise moment or decision that crosses the line or to guard against that eventuality. In words ever more true today than when first written, Alexis de Tocqueville observed more than 150 years ago:

If the lights that guide us ever go out they will fade little by little, as if of their own accord. Confining ourselves to practice, we may lose sight of basic principles, and when these have been entirely forgotten we may apply the methods derived from them badly; we might be left without the capacity to invent new methods and only able to make a clumsy and an unintelligent use of wise procedures no longer understood. (*Democracy in America,* Part II, 1840)

We must always be wary of this slippery slope upon which we may tumble toward tyranny.

It is not easy to assign a proper role to a constitution in guarding against oppression. Constitutions can be practical or they can be aspirational documents. If the latter, violations of a constitution can be tolerated more easily, for it merely sets a goal for a day in the future when an ideal society can be realized. That, the population understands, may not be in the lifetime of any now living. However, if a constitution is a practical document, it becomes one that requires the government and its people to do things "by the numbers," to follow a series of procedures that are designed to weed out bad policies. This can often be frustrating, since the process that is established can prove an obstacle to the popular will.

An enduring constitution is a real collection of a society's core values. As those values evolve, so must that constitution's reflection of them evolve; thus, the values that are embodied in a constitution must reflect basic ideals. A constitution that is weighted with specifics becomes an administrative document unworthy of the kind of respect reserved for constitutions. It instead becomes little different from regulations or ordinances, which are easily and frequently changed.

Furthermore, in the legally oriented cultures from which constitutions tend to grow, the charter must be capable of elaboration and enforcement by independent courts. Otherwise, they are mere statements, incapable of being followed and impractical in all respects. In those circumstances, they become aspirations without a practical means to achieve the carefully delineated goals of a constitution. Necessarily, when constitutions are statements of fundamental principles, their specific applications—particularly in futurity, when unforeseen circumstances call them into account—remain open to debate.

When humans organize themselves into communities—whether these societies are essentially political, social, or entrepreneurial—the individuals that constitute them find only a certain set of hierarchical values acceptable. If the individual feels oppressed, the government, the family, or the business that is the oppressor can be characterized as dictatorial. The values by which that society operates—including the liberty that is accorded the individual—constitute the governing culture for that community. That culture is made up of different tolerances in different circumstances. When all must pull together, such as during a time of war or other major crisis, the iconoclast is often not tolerated. When there is more room for creativity, the person who hears a different drummer is a more valued member of that society.

Basic to this brand of constitutionalism is the value ascribed to human dignity, the most fundamental of all constitutional concepts. If one were to put a legalistic face on the concept of human dignity, the familiar words one might use include *liberty, justice,* and *equality.* These naturally are fundamental constitutional concepts; however, if one were to choose another set of words to describe the same basic set of values, other words like *individualism, fairness,* and *self-worth* would be equally appropriate. This is why there are substantial links when one talks of constitutionalism in relation to a political society, a family, a business enterprise, or other human groupings. When humans organize themselves in these groupings, they choose the set of hierarchical values that reflect their formulation of what is required to maintain human dignity. That is what constitutionalism is all about.

Technology provides a continuing challenge to the governing culture of society. Technical advances can be liberating, but they can also be restricting. The verdict depends largely on the uses a society approves and the ones they deny to government or to any other powerful institution.

Scores of books have portrayed technology as the oppressor. To the Filipino people in 1986, it contributed to a bloodless revolution that toppled the authoritarian regime of Ferdinand Marcos. The Marcos regime had tightly controlled what appeared in the Philippine press. But a people hungry for the truth cannot be denied. Underground newspapers that challenged the official story were widely circulated. These might have easily been dismissed as more bile from malcontents who were only interested in stirring up trouble. However, another source gave the underground press new credibility: news reports from U.S. newspapers, magazines, and television broadcasts. A "video revolution" occurred, as videotapes and photocopies of U.S. news reports were smuggled into the country, copied, and distributed widely. Technology, long used against the people, provided the route to the truth.

The people were also ready to pursue the cool elixir of self-government. The Filipino people had reached a special moment in their national history in which they could either take control of their own destiny or allow themselves to continue to be buffeted indefinitely by the whims and misfortunes of autocratic rule. They opted for self-government, with all the uncertainties and difficulties it entails.

Technology today is often associated with modern communications and a world made smaller by it. We know more about each other, and it is more difficult to keep information from the worldwide public. Whether this is an inexorable trend remains to be seen, but it is an area that merits continuous reexamination. A chance to do so was the idea behind "High Technology and Human Freedom," the Ninth International Smithsonian Symposium. The symposium examined the interplay of technology and freedom in many spheres.

The essays that follow are derived from that symposium. (Others from the symposium have already appeared in a volume named after the symposium and edited by Lewis Lapham.) These essays indicate that constitutionalism is an inherent part of the human condition. In the first section, "Tyranny, Technology, and Their Control," the essayists describe the intersection of technology and constitutionalism at the nation-state level. Abbott Gleason explores the limitations of the word *totalitarianism* in understanding oppressive systems. A. E. Dick Howard argues that courts and constitutional principles should exist as vehicles to help the people achieve popular goals in the social and political realms. The late Ithiel de Sola Pool asserts that technology, rather than existing as a tool of oppression, can have a liberating effect that will benefit society as a whole and tend to cause oppressive regimes to lose ground in scientific and other advancements. David F. Linowes examines the practical educational requirements of living in a world that is becoming more reliant on computers.

"The Struggle for Constitutional Order" is a section devoted to case studies, both modern and historical. Tad Szulc describes modern Poland, Gwendolen M. Carter focuses on South Africa, and Charles F. Gallagher explores the Spanish past. Native Americans are the concern for LaDonna Harris's essay.

The final section, "Constitutionalism in Daily Life," examines other organizational units and the application of constitutional principles. José Antonio Jáuregui uses game theory to explain human behavior. The family farm and its relationship to world productivity is the topic of Orville L. Freeman's essay. The final three essays, by Gordon W. Engdahl, Leonard R. Sayles, and William Foote Whyte, examine organizational management within a corporate environment.

Whatever the relationship between humans, as citizens of a state or part of a small voluntary association, the concern for individual freedom is quite similar. It is up to the members of that society, however, to keep it vital and responsive to the changes that technology brings.

Robert S. Peck   8

1

TYRANNY, TECHNOLOGY, AND THEIR CONTROL

REFLECTIONS ON ORWELL, TOTALITARIANISM, AND *1984*

ABBOTT GLEASON

Some years ago, when people realized how close to 1984 we were getting, they began to mention it rather frequently, sometimes with a chuckle or a smirk, but I have yet to hear anything very interesting said about the arrival of this anniversary, which had been lurking in the backs of our minds for so long. As we actually rang in the new year, I checked myself out for systemic tremors, but I am still uncertain about what meaning the arrival of 1984 had, if any.

Presumably one may feel relief that we, in our Anglo-American corner of the world, have not moved further than we have in the direction of the society whose lineaments Orwell sketched forty years ago; although libertarians of the Right and Left will continue to scold us about how far gone in the loss of freedom we actually are. The intellectual Right, for whom *1984* has always been a relatively straightforward depiction of a Soviet world, will keep on warning us that the threat remains as real today as in 1949, whatever the liberals and peaceniks may say. But even if one concedes that the forces of bureaucratic despotism have made considerable strides since *1984* appeared, it seemed to me when I reread it recently that its meaning had become in some way less specific and more diffuse, and the society it depicted was less simply a composite of the Soviet and Nazi experiences than when I read it for the first time in the 1950s.

Of course, at one level it is perfectly proper to understand *1984* as a warning that what Orwell called totalitarianism could triumph as easily in the Anglo-American world as elsewhere. Orwell struck this cautionary note on several occasions himself, in attempting to clarify for his readers why he had written *1984* and what he meant by it. On June 16, 1949, for instance, he wrote to Francis A. Henson of the United Auto Workers that his novel was:

NOT intended as an attack on Socialism or the British Labour Party (of which I am a supporter) but as a show-up of the perversions to which a centralized economy is liable and which have already been realized in Communism and Fascism. I do not believe that the kind of society I describe necessarily *will* arrive, but I believe (allowing of course for the fact that the book is a satire) that something resembling it *could* arrive. I believe also that totalitarian ideas have taken root in the minds of intellectuals everywhere, and I have tried to draw these ideas out to their logical consequences. The scene of the book is laid in Britain in order to emphasize that the English-speaking races are not innately better than anyone else and that totalitarianism, *if not fought against*, could triumph anywhere.

But despite these straightforward words, the cautionary dimension of *1984* far from exhausts the meanings contained in the text. It has a demonic and visionary element that prevents us from reading it that way, whatever Orwell or anyone else may tell us. Considered from the point of view of Orwell's intellectual biography, *1984* pulls together most of the key ideas he had been developing since the early thirties. Perhaps *ideas* is the wrong word for such deeply felt fears and hunches: his revulsion at power-hungry intellectuals; his suspicion of social rationalization and centralization (combined with a steadily deepening and more explicit sympathy for the historically specific and local); and a growing fear that behind all the great ideological structures of the modern world—fascism, capitalism, communism, perhaps even socialism—lurked a violent and sadistic lust for domination. Close to the heart of Orwell's nightmare was his sense that with power-oriented intellectuals disposing of such technically sophisticated means of coercion and control, what we normally and simplemindedly speak of as "objective reality," in both past and present, might effectively disappear, dependent as it was on fallible memory and the survival of some instinct toward nonideological truth telling. Orwell understood as well as anyone ever has that ideas of rebellion as well as of conservatism must be rooted in the soil of culture and experience. If people could be deprived of their past, which is to say deprived of their ability to imagine a different life, the taproot of rebellion would be cut. No previous despot had been able to conceive of anything so grand. Orwell, both a traditionalist and a Socialist, was depressed and terrified. He never ceased to be a champion of the underdog, as he understood the matter, but he had to reject violently one of the traditional assumptions of the modern Left since it began in the Enlightenment: that the rational organization of society in the hands of secular and nontraditional "authorities" was not only a great social good in itself but also a crucial part of an emergent ethical order. No wonder Orwell has never been really persona grata to the mainstream of radical thinking since the forties, when these beliefs of his crystallized.

But the reader should examine *1984* not only in relation to the intellectual biography of its author, but also in relation to the period of its creation: the latter 1940s, that time of widespread disillusion on the Left, the onset of the cold war, the period in which the term *totalitarianism* first came into widespread use. It is a fascinating term, both because of its clarity—more apparent than real—and because its rise and decline tells us so much about changing political perceptions in the twentieth century. Whatever else it may be,

1984 is the most brilliant sketch of a totalitarian world as the generation that emerged from World War II feared it, simultaneously expressing and shaping those anxieties.

There is surprisingly little literature in English on the origins of the term *totalitarianism* and its early use. It emerged in the arguments and polemics that followed the Fascist achievement of power in Italy, but it took on the broader connotation of a radically new kind of state and society only in the midthirties. By 1940 it had come into much more common use, referring not only to a state that controlled the individual far more totally than had been possible prior to the advent of modern technology, but also with specific reference to what was similar to the Soviet, German, and Italian states and their practice.

Bertrand Russell referred extensively to totalitarianism in his 1938 book, *Power: A New Social Analysis*, and Orwell appears to have discussed the phenomenon for the first time in his review of Russell's book the following year. Russell did not attempt a definition, but it is clear that he saw German nationalism as a spiritual progenitor of totalitarianism, and he regarded as its most striking feature the assumption by the state of unprecedented economic as well as political power. It was the technological dimension to which he repeatedly returned in the course of the book: how radio, films, mass education, and the press made despotic control closer to total than it could ever have been in the past.

By the time Orwell began working on *1984*, *totalitarianism* had come into much more widespread use and denoted a society in which political power was in the hands of a dictator or "leader" and a nontraditional ruling elite; the mass of the population was not only politically powerless, but was deprived of all intellectual and cultural resources save those allowed or imposed by the state. The people in the totalitarian state were terrorized and isolated to a hitherto unprecedented degree by the government's enormously developed intelligence and police apparatus.

In dealing with the phenomenon of totalitarianism, novelists like

Orwell, and scholars too, laid particular stress on how totalitarianism (as opposed to earlier forms of despotism) had the will and capacity to invade and destroy previously unrationalized relationships: children's belief in their parents; close friendships; the love between a man and a woman. The relationship between the evil impulse and the technological means to carry it out was close, if ambiguous; Orwell (and other critics of totalitarianism) were highly suspicious of technology, if not quite willing to label it as evil. Orwell believed that few of the values he prized could be enhanced by modern technology, and he depicted its potentialities for regimentation and control with more demonic power and inventiveness than anyone else ever has.

In a totalitarian dictatorship there was no "civil society"; the state aspired to swallow everything, including private life. For the analyst, the anatomizer of totalitarian society, the subject to be studied was the means of state control, its parameters, and the new kind of life its victims were forced to lead. This insistence on the utterly atomized state of those who had to live in totalitarian societies was one of the major foci for criticism by those who subsequently proposed that there was really no such thing as totalitarianism or that it was inadequate as an analytical tool for study of the U.S.S.R. or any other actual society.

The belief that totalitarianism represented a whole new kind of social and political organization took shape in the 1930s, as intellectuals of the Left began to become disillusioned with the Soviet experiment and then to perceive, often reluctantly and with horror, that there were unmistakable parallels and points of comparison between Hitler's Germany and Stalin's Russia. In retrospect, it is clear that one could not have a real totalitarian typology until there were enough entities to study. By the midthirties, there were three important ones: the Soviet Union, Germany, and Italy. Many of those who spotted the parallels and first wrote about them had a Hegelian or a Marxist background; many had some connection with the interwar torment of Eastern and Central Europe. The horrifying prospect of an increasingly totalitarian world came originally to England and the United States as a specter of worlds associated with the Gestapo and the Comintern.

Given its nonnative status, it is perhaps ironical that the idea of totalitarianism should have struck the deepest intellectual roots in the Anglo-American political and academic world. Americans in particular entered a harrowing, dreadful, but at the same time exciting period in their history with the fall of France in 1940. Leaving the cocoon of isolationism, they were ready to be enlightened by sociological prophets, often speaking to them in a German accent. The ready acceptance of the phenomenon of totalitarianism, sometimes in rather schematic terms, by the American academic and political elite was subtly abetted by their previous reluctance to take an active part in the affairs of the world outside. And the Manichaean feelings naturally induced by the struggle against Nazi Germany attached themselves, with additional psychological passion, to the global rivalry with the Soviet Union, into which the United States plunged in the late forties. An understanding of the historical novelty of totalitarianism, as well as its sinister dynamism, was an aspect of the messianic consciousness of the American establishment for the quarter century after the Second World War. Part of the recent eclipse of the notion of totalitarianism lies in generational changes in the European and American elites, as well as in the milder climate of the Soviet Union after Stalin's death.

It was in terms of the dual experience of Nazi and Stalinist realities, as they emerged in the thirties and forties, that Orwell wrote *1984* and Hannah Arendt her brilliant and prolix essay, *The Origins of Totalitarianism*, which appeared in 1951. In 1953, Merle Fainsod produced his major study, *How Russia Is Ruled*, which attempted, with remarkable success, to reconcile an evolutionary view of Russian history with a firm belief that the Soviet Union had to be understood as a totalitarian state. Fainsod's book shaped the thinking of American academia about the Soviet Union for twenty years; for the last fifteen it has been increasingly under attack.

The audience for these works, particularly in the United States, belonged to a specific generation. For those who had fought in the war when young, or had grown up in the immediate postwar world, it was a matter of regretfully taking leave of American innocence and provinciality, of taking up the internationalist burdens of Woodrow Wilson, of learning European languages (beyond a little French or Spanish), of being able to talk to the European refugees from Hitler and Stalin on something like equal terms, of demonstrating that the United States had joined the modern world. The approved cultural attitude of the time was intellectually serious, worldly, and more cosmopolitan than the American elite had ever been before. That it was arrogant and excessively moralistic and self-confident is also hard to deny. Until recently, at least, Americans have continued to pay a price for seeing the world exclusively in terms of an East-West dualism in which we fight totalitarianism and wear the white hats.

Nevertheless, whatever the shortcomings of the vision of the world that the American elite learned after World War II, there was a broad, bipartisan, and not unrealistic agreement about the ends and means of American foreign policy, so that now, from our fragmented, post-Vietnam perspective, there seems to be something almost idyllic about the earnest, privileged, missionary world of the cold war elite. At least so it appears to me in retrospect.

During the 1960s, the civil rights issue, sixties' radicalism, and the Vietnam War shattered the cold war moral consensus, and as a result, the category of totalitarianism also came under increasing attack from those who, as putatively objective "social scientists," had to use it not in a context of ideological politics. The idea of totalitarianism (or the "totalitarian model" in the language of social science) suggested the central importance of terror in making the Soviet system work. It also suggested that the essence of the Soviet experience was the extraordinarily atomized quality of social life. In the totalitarian model, the coercive mobilization of a passive population by the government was the closest one could approach what Western political scientists call "political participation."

But after the death of Stalin and the revelations of Khrushchev, terror in the Soviet Union began to decrease or at any rate to become more subtle and implied. Social scientists began to believe that in order to understand Soviet political life one had to understand clientelistic networks, patronage, and even, in a muted way, "issues." Only a handful would go so far as to finish that sentence " . . . just as in the West," but students of Soviet politics have increasingly gravitated toward a reliance on the same analytical tools that have been used to study other industrial (and "developing") societies. Groups and their interaction are vital to the dynamics of Soviet society, and the "group approach" has become something of a rallying cry.

One will never know, thank God, how Hitler's Germany might have evolved, had the maestro lived to die of more-or-less natural causes, but it is clear that the evolution of the Soviet Union since 1953 has complicated the task of those who would like to maintain that a completely new type of state came into existence in that period. Terror and coercion play a much-diminished role in the life of Soviet citizens today, despite the continuing existence (in a peculiar sort of way) of the leader cult. Despite the formal preservation of Marxism-Leninism as the official ideology, with the passage of time the Soviet Union seems more and more understandable in terms of "traditional" categories. Nationalism, epic insecurity, the attempt to overcome "backwardness," authoritarian political cultures long in the making—combinations of these have gained ground on, if they have not eclipsed, Marxism-Leninism as the perceived source of Soviet dynamism.

Meanwhile, the debate between the dwindling band of explicit adherents of the totalitarian model and those who would like to ignore or criticize it became caught up in some of the ideological struggles of the 1980s: in the early years of the Reagan administration, one's view of the Soviet Union became more indicative of one's general beliefs. It is not that any significant group of European or American intellectuals had much positive to say about the Soviet Union. But the very attempt to compare the U.S.S.R. to other political entities in the world today seemed suspicious to conservatives like Alain Besançon of the Ecole des Hautes Etudes in Paris—a sure indication that the comparer had lost sight of the fact that the Soviet Union is not really a nation, or even a collection of nations, but a global ideological conspiracy. In conservative circles, one of the worst things that could be said of someone discussing the Soviet Union was that he or she believes it to be "a state like any other state." With Gorbachev in control, that world, for the moment at least, has receded.

To refuse to rule out studying the Soviet Union in comparative terms is not to say that Merle Fainsod's picture of a terrorized, atomized Soviet population in *How Russia Is Ruled* was wrong, or that the society Orwell depicted in *1984* has no connection with Soviet, or even Nazi, society. Orwell, Arendt, Fainsod—as well as Bertrand Russell and many others whom we do not primarily associate with defining totalitarianism—began in the late 1930s to see ways in which the regimes of Mussolini, Hitler, and Stalin were alike and were historically novel. If it presently appears that these now not-so-new but still nasty regimes have greater links with the past than was often noticed in the heyday of totalitarianism, why should anyone be surprised? After all, except to faithful Platonists, these categories are human inventions whose function is to direct our attention to some—often new—aspect of social reality. Even today, when many scholars are reluctant to use the terms *totalitarianism* and *totalitarian*, they come relatively easily to the lips of nonscholars, including a great many people who lived many years in the Soviet empire. If they want to describe the world they lived in as "totalitarian," I will not smite them with the powerful weapons of "social science."

THE SUPREME COURT AND THE LIVING CONSTITUTION

A. E. Dick Howard

The citizens of the United States live under a constitution that, drafted at Philadelphia in the summer of 1787, has endured for two hundred years. Measured by the experience of other nations, the American constitutional adventure is an anomaly. France has had five republics in the past two hundred years. A majority of the countries of the world live under constitutions written since 1970. Every year sees constitutional drafters at work in one country or another, rewriting that nation's basic law.

The story of American constitutionalism is a long one. The Constitution has its roots deep in Anglo-American history. When the framers met at Philadelphia, they were not writing on a blank slate. Several influences shaped their view of the task before them.

One influence was that of the cumulative lessons of British constitutional history. When King John, under pressure from the barons and their allies, agreed to Magna Carta, that document contained the seeds of later constitutional development. In the seventeenth century, when Parliament quarreled with the Stuart kings over revenue and other measures, those struggles had their echo in the colonies then being founded in the New World. And, toward the end of the seventeenth century, when the Glorious Revolution gave firm shape to England's constitutional order, the adoption of the English Bill of Rights offered a model for later American developments.

The Philadelphia framers were heirs, as well, to lessons derived from events on the American continent. Each of the English colonies had a charter, in which colonists were guaranteed the "privileges, franchises, and immunities" they had enjoyed in the mother country. Beginning with such events as the calling, in Virginia in 1619, of the first legislative assembly and the drafting, in Massachusetts in 1620, of the Mayflower Compact, Americans experimented with the forms of constitutionalism.

Other influences, of course, were also felt. The framers were children of the Enlightenment. Hence, American constitutional ideas owed a debt to the writings of such thinkers as Locke and Montesquieu. James Madison, through his studies at Princeton and through his own voracious reading, reflected the insights of the Scottish Enlightenment.

From the time of the Stamp Act of 1765 to the outbreak of the Revolution in 1776, Americans produced an outpouring of tracts, resolutions, pamphlets, and declarations. Attacking British policies, Americans became well versed in constitutional disputation. Moreover, well before the delegates journeyed to Philadelphia, the several states had adopted their own constitutions.

Thus, the document written in 1787—and the Bill of Rights, which was added soon thereafter—should be read and understood against this rich history of events and ideas. Nor, of course, did time stand still. The early years of the Republic saw developments—the enactment of the Judiciary Act of 1789, the rise of political parties, the storm over the Alien and Sedition Acts, among others—that affected thinking about the Constitution's meaning.

The decades after 1787 saw the American nation grow from a long strip of settlements bounded for the most part by the Alleghenies to a nation impelled by westward migration. Innovations and new technology brought the growth of industry and commerce, and pressures such as Jacksonian democracy forced politics into new patterns.

The Constitution, too, evolved. Some of the changes took the shape of formal amendments, the Bill of Rights being the earliest and most striking addition. A century later, the Civil War and Reconstruction brought, among other additions, the Fourteenth Amendment, the germ of so much modern constitutional jurisprudence.

Evolution has by no means been confined to amendments. Much of the gloss has come through judicial decisions. History takes special note of John Marshall's articulation of the Supreme Court's power to declare a statute unconstitutional, a prerogative not spelled out in the Constitution's text. Marshall also was aggressive in vindicating national interests against those of the states and in generously interpreting Congress's powers, especially through a broad reading of the "necessary and proper" clause.

In modern times, the Supreme Court has been active on many fronts. During the tenure of Chief Justice Earl Warren (1953–69), the Court offered bold judicial solutions to a range of social and political problems. Often accused by their critics of being social engineers, the justices ordered the desegregation of public schools, brought about reapportionment of state and national legislative districts, and accomplished sweeping nationalization of the rules of criminal procedure. Many of the Warren Court's decisions—*Brown v. Board of Education* (school desegregation), *Baker v. Carr* (reapportionment), *Mapp v. Ohio* (search and seizure), and *Miranda v. Arizona* (interrogations) are leading examples—are almost as well known to the laity as to lawyers and judges.

Judicial activism means an enlarged role for the courts and for constitutional norms. Americans have shown themselves willing to take an ever-widening range of issues to court. And judges appear ready to take on the task of social engineering.

Among the factors that are at work one may note the following:

(1) The rise of modern government has multiplied the opportunities for clashes between government and citizens. Administrative agencies, entitlement programs, and other aspects of the social service or welfare state blur distinctions between the public and private sectors and create occasion for litigation.

(2) The political branches at both the state and national levels often appear to fail in addressing major issues. Those who are disappointed in the political process are thus encouraged to look for other forums. The decline of the political parties has contributed to the malaise of the legislative process.

(3) The civil rights movement has set an important example for others. Blacks went to court seeking redress not elsewhere available (especially before enactment of federal civil rights and voting rights legislation). Their success led to imitation by other groups, bypassing the political process in favor of judicial action.

(4) Congress has created new causes of action or remedies. An example is the Attorney Fees Awards Act of 1976. Such acts make judicial forums more accessible and attractive.

(5) The rise of a "rights syndrome" results in the tendency to state a claim or interest as a *right*. This fuels recourse to the courts, for those who declare themselves to have a "right" at stake are less likely to wish to compromise that claim. This phenomenon is illustrated by the spread of antidiscrimination laws from race to other differences, such as gender, handicap, or sexual preference.

(6) In line with the rise of the behavioral sciences, notions about the function of law have changed. Earlier notions about law as a "brooding omnipresence"—something to be discovered as one might elaborate principles of physics—have given way to the manipulation of law as an instrument of social change. The movement called "legal realism," influential in American law schools a genera-

tion or so ago, placed particular emphasis on the role of judges as a creative force in remaking the law.

Judicial activism is a mixed blessing. Activist judicial decisions have yielded some manifestly positive accomplishments. A wider spectrum of individuals—especially those with little political power—now have enhanced access to the courts. Judicial decrees have brought more fairness in the processes of criminal justice (it is hard to fault the proposition that a criminal defendant unable to hire a lawyer ought to have one appointed). Courts have placed limits on government discretion in dealing with citizens by placing due process requirements on administrative hearings and by curbing excessive police practices.

Judicial decisions have furthered the open society. Courts have looked to the First Amendment to foster robust debate over public issues, to allow freer voice for unpopular opinions, to protect one's conscience and religious views against government intrusion, and, in general, to promote a free flow of expression in ways that enlarge both self-expression and collective choice. Likewise, personal autonomy has become a constitutional value in a way that might have gladdened the heart of John Stuart Mill.

Rulings protecting voting and equal representation have bolstered the political process. Principles of equality have been enhanced by the desegregation decisions and by other cases vindicating civil rights and rulings against racial or other forms of invidious discrimination.

For all its beneficent results, however, judicial activism has sobering implications. The power of judges has grown, both in defining substantive rights and in creating remedies. A right—the right of "privacy" comes to mind—need not be mentioned in the Constitution for a court to find it to be of constitutional dimension.

As to remedies, traditional forms of relief, such as injunctions forbidding illegal conduct, have given way to affirmative decrees, in which judges declare what course of action officials must pursue. In institutional litigation, judges become overseers of public institutions such as prisons and mental hospitals. In the 1960s, District Judge Frank M. Johnson, Jr., was issuing so many decrees of this kind against state institutions that he came to be called "the real governor of Alabama."

All in all, the Constitution and the courts have become vehicles for solving major social and political issues. Many of the most controversial issues debated in the legislative chambers and in the hustings are those revolving around judicial decisions—abortion, prayers in schools, and busing among them.

When one hears praise of the "living Constitution," it is this use of constitutional norms by courts to achieve reform that is often in the speaker's mind. To the extent that judges go beyond the explicit text of the Constitution to reach a result based on some intuitive sense of fairness, decency, or right, their rulings recall the historical interplay between the tradition of constitutionalism and that of the natural law.

In the tracts and resolves complaining of British policy in the 1760s and the 1770s, the American colonists often appealed both to natural rights and to the British Constitution. As Massachusetts's Samuel Adams said, "Magna Carta itself is in substance but a declaration in the name of King, Lords, and Commons of the sense the latter had of their original, inherent, and indefeasible natural Rights."

This eclecticism, this appeal to competing sources of jurisprudence, has shaped constitutional interpretation from that time to our own. One has but to read the angry clashes of Justices Hugo L. Black and Felix Frankfurter, for example, in their respective opinions in *Adamson v. California* (1947). Such debates reveal how contemporary is the dispute over appeals to language, text, and framers' intention and the use of extratextual sources.

Another tension arises from two basic, but often conflicting, assumptions of the American constitutional system. One tenet of constitutionalism in America is politically accountable decision making. This principle is reflected in notions about democracy and majority rule. Constitutional government connotes decisions by officials accountable to the body of the electorate.

Another basic tenet, however, is countermajoritarian. A concept of individual rights, especially one grounded in Enlightenment notions of natural rights and a social compact, invites the creation of a device to secure those rights. It suggests the need for a forum, independent of popular pressures, for the vindication of rights, especially those spelled out in a bill of rights. Judicial review becomes the device, and the courts the forum, often working to thwart the will of a majority, even when reflected in normal legislative processes.

In exercising its powers of judicial review, the Supreme Court has become an arena for resolving fundamental issues in political theory and morality. Where political theorists have long disputed, the justices have entered. They have proved willing to choose among competing theories of politics and government. Thus, in *Reynolds v. Sims* (1964), the majority elevated the one-person, one-vote formula over other principles of representation, much to the consternation of Justice John Marshall Harlan, who, in dissent, complained that the Constitution did not oblige the states to choose one theory of representation over another.

Similarly, where philosophers and theologians have failed to agree, the justices have acted. They have decided questions of life and death in such decisions as the 1973 abortion decision, *Roe v. Wade*. The several opinions in the first major capital punishment case, *Furman v. Georgia* (1972), find the justices debating issues familiar to philosophers, such as the question of whether retribution is a permissible basis for punishment. At times the Supreme Court seems to behave as the country's moral tutor.

The result is a dialectic between the Court and the other branches of the federal government, the states, and public attitudes. Some of the Court's opinions "take" and are accepted by the public. Such clearly was the case with the reapportionment decisions. Some legislators (especially those likely to be the losers in the redrawing of district boundaries) protested the Court's decisions, but most citizens could find little quarrel with the notion that one person's vote ought to be worth no more than another's.

Some opinions engender broad opposition. In antebellum days, abolitionists ignored *Dred Scott*, and in the twentieth century, southern legislators embarked on a course of "massive resistance" after *Brown v. Board of Education*. Prolife groups continue to proclaim the illegitimacy of *Roe v. Wade*, and fundamentalist religionists are not content to abide a jurisprudence of the "wall of separation" of church and state in such areas as public education.

Commonly there is a testing of limits. Although the basic premise of *Brown* has now reached the level of acceptance of the most sturdy of constitutional decisions, its ultimate implementation continues to embroil federal district courts, especially where school busing has been an issue. Prolife forces continue to enact laws and ordinances intended to limit access to abortions, seeking test cases and hoping to see *Roe* undermined or abandoned.

Sometimes the result is uneasy, often instable doctrines—something for one side, something for the other. The Supreme Court's famous decision in *Bakke*, the Court's first important affirmative action case (1978), left both sides proclaiming victory—Allan Bakke, because he gained admittance to the University of California's medical school at Davis, and supporters of affirmative action, because the Court left ways for such programs, if designed with care, to be validated. In the abortion case, the Court has stood by *Roe* where direct burdens (such as waiting periods or consent requirements) are placed in the path of women wanting abortions, but the justices have permitted Congress and the states to cut off funding for abortions.

Reflective students of the judicial process—laypeople as well as lawyers—are obliged to weigh the costs and benefits of resorting to the courts to resolve social and political issues. The gains include a more open society—readier access to the ballot, fuller rights of speech and expression, more personal autonomy, limits on government arbitrariness and discretion. But there are risks. The cumulative effect of shifting decisions to a nonaccountable branch of government can undermine the vitality of a democracy.

We seek twin goals. One is the benefit of the open society. The other is education in the civic virtues that nurture responsible citizenship. An activist judiciary can, if it acts with prudence and restraint, promote the health of the body politic by strengthening the conditions within which a free people can shape their own future. But that same activism can dull the sense of responsibility and choice that lies at the base of free institutions.

In *1984* George Orwell warned of the consequences of totalitarian rule. By and large, the Supreme Court has used the Constitution to help the American people steer away from the bleak picture Orwell painted. But in the justices' library, alongside Orwell, should repose other books—the Federalist papers, the debates on the Constitution's ratification, the musings of the founders and the great jurists of American history. Judges are not knights, sworn to some great crusade. Their intervention should be the exception, not the rule. They operate, ideally, in aid of responsible choices by an informed citizenry, not in place of them.

SPEECH IN AN ELECTRONIC AGE

ITHIEL DE SOLA POOL

Civil liberty functions today in a changing technological context. For five hundred years a struggle was fought, and in a few countries won, for the right of people to speak and print freely, unlicensed, uncensored, and uncontrolled. But new technologies of electronic communication may now regulate old and freed media such as pamphlets, platforms, and periodicals to a corner of the public forum. Electronic modes of communication that enjoy lesser rights are moving to center stage. The new communication technologies have not inherited all the legal immunities that were won for the old. When wires, radio waves, satellites, and computers became major vehicles of discourse, regulation seemed to be a technical necessity. And so, as speech increasingly flows over those electronic media, the five-century growth of an unabridged right of citizens to speak without controls may be endangered.

Alarm over this trend is common, though understanding of it is rare. In 1980 the chairman of the American Federal Communications Commission (FCC) sent a shiver through print journalists when he raised the question of whether a newspaper delivered by teletext is an extension of print and thus as free as any other newspaper, or whether it is a broadcast and thus under the control of the government. A reporter, discussing computerized information services, broached an issue with far-reaching implications for society when she asked, "Will traditional First Amendment freedom of the press apply to the signals sent out over telephone wires or television cables?" William S. Paley, chairman of the Columbia Broadcasting System (CBS), warned the press: "Broadcasters and print people have been so busy improving and defining their own turf that it has escaped some of us how much we are being drawn together by the vast revolution in 'electronification' that is changing the face of the media today. . . . Convergence of delivery mechanisms for news and information raises anew some critical First Amendment questions. . . . Once the print media comes into the home through the television set, or an attachment, with an impact and basic content similar to that which the broadcasters now deliver, then the question of government regulation becomes paramount for print as well." And Senator Bob Packwood proposed a new amendment to the Constitution extending First Amendment rights to the electronic media, on the assumption that they are not covered now.

Although the first principle of communications law in the United States is the guarantee of freedom in the First Amendment, in fact this country has a trifurcated communications system. In three domains of communication—print, common carriage, and broadcasting—the law has evolved separately, and in each domain with but modest relation to the others.

In the domain of print and other means of communication that existed in the formative days of the nation, such as pulpits, periodicals, and public meetings, the First Amendment truly governs. In well over one hundred cases dealing with publishing, canvassing, public speeches, and associations, the Supreme Court has applied the First Amendment to the media that existed in the eighteenth century.

In the domain of common carriers, which includes the telephone, the telegraph, the postal system, and now some computer networks, a different set of policies has been applied, designed above all to ensure universal service and fair access by the public to the facilities of the carrier. That right of access is what defines a common carrier: it is obligated to serve all on equal terms without discrimination.

Finally, in the domain of broadcasting, Congress and the courts have established a highly regulated regime, very different from that of print. On the grounds of a supposed scarcity of usable frequencies in the radio spectrum, broadcasters are selected by the government for merit in its eyes, assigned a slice each of the spectrum of frequencies, and required to use that assignment fairly and for community welfare as defined by state authorities. The principles of common carriage and of the First Amendment have been applied to broadcasting only in atrophied form. For broadcasting, a politically managed system has been invented.

The electronic modes of twentieth-century communication, whether they be carriers or broadcasters, have lost a large part of the eighteenth- and nineteenth-century constitutional protections of no prior restraint, no licenses, no special taxes, no regulations, and no laws. Every radio spectrum user, for example, must be licensed. This requirement started in 1912, almost a decade before the beginning of broadcasting, at a time when radio was used mainly for maritime communication. Because the United States Navy's communications were suffering interference, Congress, in an effort at remedy, imposed licensing on transmitters, thereby breaching a tradition that went back to John Milton against requiring licenses for communicating.

Regulation as a response to perceived technical problems has now reached the point where transmissions enclosed in wires or cables, and therefore causing no over-the-air interference, are also licensed and regulated. The FCC claims the right to control which broadcast stations a cablecaster may or must carry. Until the courts blew the whistle, the rules even barred a pay channel from performing movies that were more than three or less than ten years old. Telephone bills are taxed. A public network interconnecting computers must be licensed and, according to present interpretations of the 1934 Communications Act, may be denied a license if the government does not believe that it serves "the public convenience, interest, or necessity."

Civil libertarians as well as free marketers are perturbed at the expanding scope of communications regulation. After computers became linked by communications networks, for example, the FCC spent several years figuring out how to avoid regulating the computer industry. The line of reasoning behind this laudable self-restraint, known as deregulation, has nothing to do, however, with freedom of speech. Deregulation, whatever its economic merits, is something much less than the First Amendment. The Constitution, in Article I, Section 8, gives the federal government the right to regulate interstate commerce, but in the First Amendment, equally explicitly, it excludes one kind of commerce, namely acts of communication, from government authority. Yet here is the FCC trying to figure out how it can avoid regulating the commerce of the computer industry (an authority Congress could have given but never did) while continuing to regulate communications whenever it considers this necessary. The Constitution has been turned on its head.

The mystery is how the clear intent of the Constitution, so well and strictly enforced in the domain of print, has been so neglected in the electronic revolution. The answer lies partly in changes in the prevailing concerns and historical circumstances from the time of the founding fathers to the world of today; but it also lies at least as much in the failure of Congress and the courts to understand the character of the new technologies. Judges and legislators have tried to fit technological innovations under conventional legal concepts. The errors of understanding by these nonscientific laypeople, though honest, have been mammoth. They have sought to guide toward good purposes technologies they did not comprehend.

"It would seem," wrote Alexis de Tocqueville, "that if despotism were to be established among the democratic nations of our days . . . it would be more extensive and more mild; it would degrade men without tormenting them." This is the kind of mild but degrading erosion of freedom that our system of communications faces today, not a rise of dictators or totalitarian movements. The threat in America, as Tocqueville perceived, is from well-intentioned policies, with results that are poorly foreseen. The danger is "tutelary power," which aims at the happiness of the people but also seeks to be the "arbiter of that happiness."

Yet in a century and a half since Tocqueville wrote, the mild despotism that he saw in the wings of American politics has not become a reality. For all his understanding of the American political system, he missed one vital element of the picture. In the tension between tutelary and libertarian impulses that is built into American culture, a strong institutional dike has held back assaults on freedom. It is the first ten amendments to the Constitution. Extraordinary as this may seem, in Tocqueville's great two volumes there is nowhere a mention of the Bill of Rights!

The erosion of traditional freedoms that has occurred, as government has striven to cope with problems of new communications media, would not have surprised Tocqueville, for it is a story of how, in pursuit of the public good, a growing structure of controls has been imposed. But one part of the story would have surprised him, for it tells how a legal institution that he overlooked, namely the First Amendment, has up to now maintained the freedom and individuality that he saw as endangered.

A hundred and fifty years from now, today's fears about the future of free expression may prove as alarmist as Tocqueville's did. But there is reason to suspect that our situation is more ominous. What has changed in twentieth-century communications is the technological base. Tocqueville wrote in a pluralistic society of small enterprises where the then-new mass media consisted entirely of the printed press, which the First Amendment protected.

In the period since his day, new and mostly electronic media have proliferated in the form of great oligopolistic networks of common carriers and broadcasters. Regulation was a natural response. Fortunately and strangely, as electronics advances further, another reversal is now taking place, toward decentralization and toward fragmentation of the audience of the newest communications media. The transitional era of giant media may nonetheless leave a permanent set of regulatory practices implanted on a system that is coming to have technical characteristics that would otherwise be conducive to freedom.

The causal relationships between technology and culture are a matter that social scientists have long debated. Some may question how far technological trends shape the political freedom or control under which communication takes place, believing, as does Daniel Bell, that each subsystem of society, such as techno-economics, polity, and culture, has its own heritage and axial principles and goes its own way. Others, like Karl Marx or Ruth Benedict, contend that a deep commonality binds all aspects of a culture. Some argue that technology is neutral, used as the culture demands; others that the technology of the medium controls the message.

The interaction over the past two centuries between the changing technologies of communication and the practice of free speech, I would argue, fits a pattern that is sometimes described as "soft technological determinism." Freedom is fostered when the means of communication are dispersed, decentralized, and easily available, as are printing presses or microcomputers. Central control is more likely when the means of communication are concentrated, monopolized, and scarce, as are great broadcasting networks. But the relationship between technology and institutions is not simple or unidirectional, nor are the effects immediate. Institutions that evolve in response to one technological environment persist and to some degree are later imposed on what may be a changed technology. The First Amendment came out of a pluralistic world of small communicators, but it shaped the present treatment of national networks. Later on, systems of regulation that emerged for national common carriers and for the use of "scarce" spectrum for broadcasting tended to be imposed on more recent generations of electronic technologies that no longer require them.

Simple versions of technological determinism fail to take account of the differences in the way things happen at different stages in the life cycle of a technology. When a new invention is made, such as the telephone or radio, its fundamental laws are usually not well understood. It is designed to suit institutions that already exist, but in its early stages, if it is to be used at all, it must be used in whatever form it proved experimentally to work. Institutions for its use are thus designed around a technologically determined model. Later, when scientists have comprehended the fundamental theory, the early technological embodiment becomes simply a special case. Alternative devices can then be designed to meet human needs; technology no longer need control. A 1920s motion picture had to be black and white, silent, pantomimic, and shown in a place of public assembly; there was no practical choice. A 1980s video can have whatever colors, sounds, and three-dimensional or synthetic effects are wanted and can be seen in whatever location is desired. In the meantime, however, an industry has established studios, theaters, career lines, unions, funding, and advertising practices, all designed to use the technology that is in place. Change occurs, but the established institutions are a constraint on its direction and pace.

Today, in an era of advanced (and still advancing) electronic theory, it has become possible to build virtually any kind of communications device that one might wish, though at a price. The market, not technology, sets most limits. For example, technology no longer imposes licensing and government regulation. That pattern was established for electronic media a half-century ago, when there seemed to be no alternative, but those institutions of control persist. That is why today's alarms could turn out to be more portentous than Tocqueville's.

The key technological change, at the root of the social changes, is that communication, other than conversation face to face, is becoming overwhelmingly electronic. Not only is electronic communications growing faster than traditional print media, but also the convergance of modes of delivery is bringing the press, journals, and books into the electronic world. One question raised by these changes is whether some social features are inherent in the electronic character of the emerging media. Is television the model of the future? Are electromagnetic pulses simply an alternative conduit to deliver whatever is wanted, or are there aspects of electronic technology that make it different from print—more centralized or more decentralized, more banal or more profound, more private or more government dependent?

The electronic transformation of the media occurs not in a vacuum but in a specific historical and legal context. Freedom for publishing has been one of America's proudest traditions. But just what is it that the courts have protected, and how does this differ from how the courts acted later, when the media through which ideas flowed came to be the telegraph, telephone, television, or computers? What images did policymakers have of how each of these media works; how far were their images valid; and what happened to their images when the facts changed?

In each of the three parts of the American communications system—print, common carriers, and broadcasting—the law has rested on a perception of technology that is sometimes accurate, often inaccurate, and which changes slowly as technology changes quickly. Each new advance in the technology of communications disturbs a status quo. It meets resistance from those whose dominance it threatens, but if useful, it begins to be adopted. Initially, because it is new and a full scientific mastery of the options is not yet at hand, the invention comes into use in a clumsy form. Technical laypeople, such as judges, perceive the new technology in that early, awkward form, which then becomes their image of its nature, possibilities, and use. This perception is an incubus on later understanding.

The courts and regulatory agencies in the American system (or other authorities elsewhere) enter as arbiters of the conflicts among entrepreneurs, interest groups, and political organizations battling for control of the new technology. The arbiters, applying familiar analogies from the past to their lay image of the new technology, create a partly old, partly new structure of rights and obligations. The telegraph was analogized to railroads, the telephone to the telegraph, and cable television to broadcasting. The legal system thus invented for each new technology may in some instances, like the First Amendment, be a tour de force of political creativity, but in other instances it may be less suitable. The system created can turn out to be inappropriate to more habile forms of the technology, which gradually emerge as the technology progresses. This is when problems arise, as they are arising so acutely today.

Historically, the various media that are now converging have been differently organized and differently treated under the law. The outcome to be feared is that communications in the future may be unnecessarily regulated under the unfree tradition of law that has been applied so far to the electronic media. The clash between the print, common carrier, and broadcast models is likely to be a vehement communications policy issue in the next decades. Convergence of modes is upsetting the trifurcated system developed over the past two hundred years, and questions that had seemed to be settled centuries ago are being reopened, unfortunately sometimes not in a libertarian way.

The problem is worldwide. What is true for the United States is true, *mutatis mutandis,* for all free nations. All have the same three systems. All are in their way deferential to private publishing but allow government control or ownership of carriers and broadcasters. And all are moving into the era of electronic communications. So they face the same prospect of either freeing up their electronic media or else finding their major means of communications slipping back under political control.

The American case is unique only in the specific feature of the

First Amendment and in the role of the courts in upholding it. The First Amendment, as interpreted by the courts, provides an anchor for freedom of the press and thus accentuates the difference between publishing and the electronic domain. Because of the unique power of the American courts, the issue in the United States unfolds largely in judicial decisions. But the same dilemmas and trends could be illustrated by citing declarations of policy and institutional structures in each advanced country.

If the boundaries between publishing, broadcasting, cable television, and the telephone network are indeed broken in the coming decades, then communications policies in all advanced countries must address the issue of which of the three models will dominate public policy regarding them. Public interest regulation could begin to extend over the print media as those media increasingly use regulated electronic channels. Conversely, concern for the traditional notion of a free press could lead to finding ways to free the electronic media from regulation. The policies adopted, even among free nations, will differ, though with plenty in common. The problems in all of them are much the same.

The electronic information marketplace of the future will provide a variety of delivery vehicles and forms of information display. The content that publishers will offer over these vehicles will be in voice and video, in addition to text. The messages delivered can at some cost be multimedia spectaculars, but even at low cost they can mix audio and visuals with text. Today one can buy a book or magazine, perhaps beefed up with pictures, and one can buy a cassette or disk of a movie, perhaps clarified with captions; but electronic technology will create options for mixes not yet dreamed of. Entrants into electronic publishing may therefore come from many directions—not only from book, magazine, and newspaper publishing, but also from cablecasting, television, Hollywood, the computer industry, and the telecommunications industry. As long as all these vigorous competitors can obtain access to the major carriers, monopoly among electronic publishers will not arise easily.

Although paper will not vanish, electronic publishing may in the long run evolve to something radically different from what we know today. Though pluralistic, competitive, and economical, like print, it may differ markedly in content from what is now found in magazines, newspapers, and books. Automobiles looked like horseless carriages at the start but not forever; it may be the same with electronic publishing.

As computers become the printing presses of the twenty-first century, ink marks on paper will continue to be read, and broadcasts to be watched, but other new major media will evolve from what are now but the toys of computer hackers. Videodisks, integrated memories, and data bases will serve functions that books and libraries now serve, and information retrieval systems will serve for what magazines and newspapers do now. Networks of satellites, optical fibers, and radio waves will serve the functions of the present-day postal system. Speech will not be free if these are not also free.

The danger is not of an electronic nightmare, but of human error. It is not computers but policy that threatens freedom. The censorship that followed the printing press was not entailed in Gutenberg's process; it was a reaction to it. The regulation of electronic communication is likewise not entailed in its technology but is a reaction to it. Computers, telephones, radio, and satellites are technologies of freedom, as much as was the printing press.

The technologies used for self-expression, human intercourse, and recording of knowledge are in unprecedented flux. A panoply of electronic devices puts at everyone's hand capacities far beyond anything that the printing press could offer. Machines that think, that bring great libraries into anybody's study, that allow discourse among persons a half-world apart, are expanders of human culture. They allow people to do anything that could be done with the communications tools of the past, and many more things too.

It is important to note the increasing sophistication of the equipment on the user's own premises. Since the output and input of networks may be printed on paper, shown on a screen, or declaimed in sound, the equipment needed on the user's premises will be costly. Although the costs of computer logic, memory, and long-distance communication are falling, the uses that people want to make of them are expanding even faster. A $4,000 microcomputer can today do things that would have required a million-dollar computer a few years ago, when few would have predicted that millions of ordinary people would spend $4,000 for that home gadget. In the future, many millions of households will similarly desire large-size, high-definition screens, cameras to originate video, and large memory devices to retain libraries of information for work and pleasure.

This trend favors decentralization. There is no reason to assume that the communications network of the future will be a single large organization with a central brain. It may be so, but it need not be. Having a hierarchical structure governed by a central brain is only one way to organize complex systems. A human being is organized that way; so is a nation-state. But the capitalist economy is not, nor is the complex system of scientific knowledge, nor is the ecological system of the biosphere. For an uncentralized system to function, there must be some established ways of interconnecting the parts other than by command; the interconnections may be managed by conventions, habits, or Darwinian processes. Capitalist property rights are enforced by laws; language is enforced by custom; creatures in the biosphere do not survive if they cannot metabolize other species.

The future of society rests on the free flow of information through the new communications system. The exchanges that occur through that system will serve human achievement in a way that a closed society cannot. The race to advance technology may actually require the freedoms that result from decentralization. Technology will not be to blame if Americans fail to encompass this system within the political tradition of free speech. On the contrary, electronic technology is conducive to freedom.

The issue of how to handle the electronic media is the salient free-speech problem for this decade, at least as important for this moment as were the last generation's issues for them, and as the next generation's will be for them too. But perhaps it is more than that. The move to electronic communications may be a turning point that history will remember. Just as in seventeenth- and eighteenth-century Great Britain and America a few tracts and acts set precedents for print by which we live today, so what we think and do today may frame the information system for a substantial period in the future.

In that future society, the norms that govern information and communications will be even more crucial than in the past. Those who read, wrote, and published in the seventeenth and eighteenth centuries, and who shaped whatever heritage of art, literature, science, and history continues to matter today, were part of a small minority, well under one-tenth of the work force. Information activities now occupy the lives of much of the population. In advanced societies about half the work force are information processors. It would be dire if the laws we make today governing the dominant mode of information handling in such an information society were subversive of its freedom. The onus is on us to determine whether free societies in the twenty-first century will conduct electronic communication under the conditions of freedom established for the domain of print through centuries of struggle, or whether that great achievement will become lost in a confusion about new technologies.

COMPUTERS AND THE LEARNING ENVIRONMENT: TASKS FOR TEACHERS, PARENTS, AND INDUSTRY

DAVID F. LINOWES

Computers are causing a revolution in education as profound as that caused by the printing press. The impact is compounded by several factors: the absence of public awareness of technology's unrelenting seepage into our learning environments; the lack of social, economic, and political planning by government, business, and academic leaders; and the relative insensitivity of electronics scientists to the all-embracing implications inherent in the revolution they are creating. Scientists tell us that the technology currently in place is one hundred years behind what is already available. They talk of entire libraries held on a single silicon chip, of all of a factory's controls placed on one silicon wafer.

The chip made of silicon, which next to oxygen is the most abundant element on earth, is probably the most important technological development in this century. Its application to the computer enables that electronic miracle to perform tasks previously reserved for the human mind.

Two decades ago, it would have been impossible to computerize the game of chess. The first three moves on each side would have required a machine the size of a cigar box. By the sixth move, the machine would have needed an area the size of Manhattan. In other words, the size of the set had to be proportionate to the number of possibilities to be accommodated, and beyond the tenth move the choices expand into the millions. Today, an electronic chess machine the size of a cigar box can play complete games—as many as sixty moves.

It is always difficult to grasp and convey the significance of a technological trend that is progressing at an exponential rate and shows no sign of letting up. An analogy with a more familiar technological development might help. If jet travel technology had developed at the same rate as the computer has in the past twenty-five years, we would be traveling to Europe in seven minutes at a cost of two cents in an airplane the size of a shoe box.

This same technology is giving computers the capacity to learn, enabling them to enlarge the human mind's horizons or even to displace the mind in many tasks. Just as machines have been an extension of a person's limbs and muscles, the computer is becoming an extension of one's mind and memory.

We have learned more about the human brain in the last ten years than we have known through the rest of history. With that knowledge, the brain is now being recreated in computers. This new ultrasophisticated software, or "artificial intelligence," is being used to solve complex mathematical problems and to make medical diagnoses. Researchers at IBM and Texas Instruments are using artificial intelligence to analyze geographical formations, design new biological genes, and to read, digest, and answer correspondence.

Computers are being programmed to duplicate the decision-making process of leading experts in several fields. These "expert" programs are designed by programming all known information on a given subject into the computer. Programmers then interview recognized experts in the field to determine how they process information to form judgments. That process is then also programmed into the same computer.

Stanford University researchers have developed a program called Eurisko that enables a computer to develop its own theories and ideas once it is given the principles of a discipline. At Yale, scientists have computers interpreting newspaper articles that are read with optical scanning devices. One program correlates stories about terrorism and is becoming an expert at knowing what terrorists want and need. Eventually, researchers expect that computers will become voracious readers, constantly updating their reservoirs of knowledge.

A number of companies are marketing devices capable of synthesizing words. By the end of the 1980s, computers will be able to understand complete sentences so that typewriters can take dictation. IBM has a machine called EPISTLE (Executive-Principle's Intelligent System for Text and Linguistic Endeavors) that reads mail, understands and summarizes its contents, and replies on its own. Hewlett-Packard has an intelligent electronic mail system that forwards messages and monitors responses.

In the coming decade, people will talk to computers the same way they do with one another. A number of computers already communicate in written English. To give computers fluency, researchers at the University of Illinois, Yale, and IBM are programming the machines with two types of knowledge. First, they instruct the computer on rules of grammar and syntax. Then, they give the computer some knowledge about the world.

By the mid-1990s, the Japanese Ministry of International Trade and Industry expects to have a thinking computer. It will understand natural speech, read written language, and translate documents. The machine will draw inferences and make its own judgments. It will learn by studying its errors.

The computer is being educated! It is acquiring unorganized and unrelated facts, what we commonly recognize as *information*. It is being taught knowledge, that is, extensive facts in a particular field just as occurs in any specialized profession. And now, through "artificial intelligence," it is acquiring wisdom: knowledge of people and human life so as to produce sound judgments. It is inevitable that the computer and our educational system must become as one. The computer must be recognized as being much more than just another teaching tool. It is becoming a teaching and learning partner.

Nowhere is the clash between technological development and societal impact more acute than in the field of education. In principle, the computer offers the prospect of enormous strides in the learning ability of everyone in society. In practice, the implementation of widespread computerized learning is posing a number of severe problems that are only just being recognized by educators and policymakers.

The application of the computer to education in this nation has been spotty, but nevertheless impressive. There are more than three hundred thousand classroom computers available to students. By 1983, one out of every three public schools had computers. Standard instructional programs in most subjects are widely available for schools with the appropriate hardware.

Children as young as three or four are being introduced to computers with the aid of LOGO, a simple computer language invented by Professor Seymour Papert of the Massachusetts Institute of Technology. This system allows children to instruct a computer to design any object (a house, plane, or truck, for example) line by line on a video screen. It is believed that children who play with computers in LOGO will teach themselves mathematics as easily and naturally as they would learn to speak French by living in France.

LOGO is being implemented in a number of schools across the country. Results have shown that use of the computer has inspired a new enthusiasm and sense of discovery by teachers and pupils alike. A program developed in a number of New York schools is especially innovative. In one Manhattan school, dozens of students voluntarily flock to the school's fifth-floor computer room, at lunchtime and before or after classes, to use its Apple, Atari, and Texas Instruments machines.

One can glimpse into the future of education at an experimental private school of 120 students in Utah. Ranging from kindergarten to fifth grade, students use the computer as others use books and a blackboard. At the back of a typical classroom are several word processors, on which the children practice their language skills by themselves. They do so by sending messages to children on the other side of the world. They are part of an electronic pen-pal system with several other countries. When all the equipment is in place, the system will be able to accommodate 450 students a day. Another area the school is exploring is the use of video games for educational purposes. Such games are seen as valuable in overcoming problems of student motivation. With such applications of computers, it is expected that children will become better thinkers—more logical, better able to write as well as to compute, more confident in their own abilities, and better able to break down the problems into manageable segments.

The radical changes that are going on in education are not being initiated by the teachers or the institutions of which they are a part, but by the computer industry, students, and parents. It is the fascination of the youngsters with the new technologies in computers and telecommunications, triggered by computer companies, that is sparking their imagination and excitement to learn. Parents are pushing the schools to place computer literacy into the curricula for fear their children will be left behind. Administrators and teachers are accepting the combined leadership of industry and parents and are adjusting their learning institutions to these initiatives.

Teachers have a unique opportunity to seize upon this phenomenon and once more exercise their full authority and prestige to lead our schools to new and heightened goals tied to electronic communications equipment. It can never be forgotten, however, that computer literacy is of no avail without literacy in the arts and sciences.

At the college level, Carnegie-Mellon University will begin introducing a distributed computing network that will eventually provide the entire campus community with access to personal computers twenty to one hundred times more powerful than the average home computer. Rollins College in Florida is making computer literacy a graduation requirement.

One of the most advanced computerized educational systems in the nation was developed at the University of Illinois. PLATO (Programmed Logic for Automatic Teaching Operations) now has some two hundred university sites on the network, in this country and abroad. The system is in the process of being modified in order to increase its capacity a hundredfold. By using a system of minicomputers below the central coordinating machine, the number of terminals available from this cluster system will rise from 1,200 to around 150,000.

In the long run, the concept of "going to school" may become obsolete. If education can be successfully accomplished through computer programs and individual terminals, why not educate students at home? Home computers are already a major industry. There is no technical barrier to achieving a complete educational experience from a computer in one's own living room. The software to learn virtually any subject is now readily available. As a result, parents too are inextricably involved in the revolution that is taking place in the nation's educational systems. They too must become computer literate.

Atari has already introduced what is called "the world's first electronic university." Through its Telelearning system, it has instructors for 170 initial courses, including courses in art, finance, and business management. This computer system enables human instructors to teach one-on-one courses through personal computers over telephone lines. The concept of a school building or campus may become increasingly obsolete. More than a decade ago, some of the more imaginative educators were speaking of eliminating the "social addiction" to attending school. Proposals have been made for a deschooled world that would replace formal classes with networks of "learning exchanges." Instead of confining formal learning to the classroom, students would be taught wherever they might be: at home, at the workplace, or at the playground. People of any age who wanted to learn something would go to a counselor, somewhat as they go to a reference librarian today.

Just as the inventions of writing and the printing press necessitated the reformulation of pedagogic philosophy and technique, so the current technological advances will require the same careful reexamination of means, purpose, and policy in education. Those in education expressing concerns about the onslaught of the computer into the halls of learning should recall that twenty-four hundred years ago, when writing was invented, the educators of that day were alarmed that writing would diminish the students' interest in learning. They argued students would refuse to memorize information anymore because knowledge would always be available to them on a written document. (Do we not sense some of that kind of concern about students' pocket calculators?)

One of the more intractable problems for policymakers concerns equality of opportunity. Presently, instructional technology is concentrated in wealthy school districts. According to Market Data Retrieval, 80 percent of the nation's two thousand largest and richest public high schools have at least one microcomputer, but 60 percent of the two thousand poorest have none. Thus, computer literacy is heavily dependent upon socioeconomic factors. The danger of creating a technologically deprived class of youngsters is acute.

The paucity of effective teaching software is another problem. Much of it does not take advantage of the many capabilities of the expensive hardware that schools buy. Many of the software programs are still asking students to add two numbers and then telling them whether the answer is right or wrong. The capabilities of the hardware have hardly begun to be exploited by the simple, unimaginative, and often gimmicky software presently marketed. A recent report by the congressional Office of Technology Assessment found that what is sold today is "in general, not very good," and added that "the provision of high quality, reasonably-priced educational software is the principal technological challenge" of the day.

Modern software educational offerings, some thirty years after the development of computer-assisted instruction, should not be judged too harshly, however. No one could have predicted the present status of books in the learning process thirty years after the development of the printing press. Some responsibility for the gimmicky educational software presently available must be assumed by the computer industry. As Lewis Branscomb, vice-president and chief scientist at IBM, recently stated, his industry has aggressively sought the educational market, often "shoving things down the throats of the schools." Selling hardware to school districts that have not been trained to use it is not helpful. The National Science Board recently reported that these purchases have resulted in considerable underutilization of expensive equipment. School districts that stretch their budgets and neglect other important areas to buy the equipment are poorly served.

The various kinds of computers and related hardware and software sold by computer companies, as they scramble for markets in the schools, the home, and the workplace, are often incompatible. A company's eagerness to promote its product often causes it to design its own equipment and software. This is frequently done without consulting the appropriate educators, thereby neglecting important educational goals.

Computers being purchased for the home, schools, and other learning centers should follow a basic design, so that they are compatible with one another at least within a school district. The organized teaching profession can assert its leadership within each community by charting the direction of computer utilization, both for students and for their parents, linking schools, home, and workplace for the common good.

David F. Linowes   52

As computers increasingly infiltrate the classroom and the lives of all of us, conscious attention must be paid to human values. All human relationships include moral and ethical traits. Teachers bring such values into the classroom, injecting them into every subject we teach. When a student learns a subject from a computer, however, human values are absent. Educators will have to make conscious efforts to fill this void. Learning must not exclude the moral facets of human existence. Science and the machines it creates are neutral; they give us tools but do not tell us how to use them.

The communication of knowledge through individual terminals plugged into a computer dramatically enlarges a teacher's capacity—hundreds of students can be taught at one time, instead of thirty. The extension of a teacher's effectiveness need no longer be limited to a classroom or a school. It can be extended to everyone interested in learning, wherever they might be. Exciting challenges, as well as economic rewards, lie ahead for the teaching profession, as a consequence. Just as the machine during the Industrial Revolution brought previously unheard-of pay scales to the industrial worker, so too can the computer make the economic rewards of teaching surge.

Business, government, and other institutions increasingly are establishing and maintaining huge data banks accessible by personal terminals. This same information is needed by a universe of people: educators, researchers, students, and the general public. Could not a master data bank be created, linking the various independent data banks into a cooperative project for all to access under the auspices of a region's learning institutions? What a great challenge and opportunity this could be for educators, librarians, and museum curators! Leaders in the teaching profession joining with computer industry executives could point the way.

To expedite such developments, the Secretary of Education, working with national educational institutions, should design a national public policy agenda for computer literacy to make the computer a part of the learning environment for everyone. Mayors and governors together with local schools, libraries, and museums could serve as catalysts and stimulants for bringing together industry, school, and the home to promote adoption of appropriate hardware and software. Parent-teacher associations could serve as clearing centers to ensure the compatibility of computing hardware purchased by parents and by educational institutions. Where necessary, all should join in aggressively seeking funding to supplement school budgets for poor neighborhoods so that youngsters in less affluent communities are not informationally disenfranchised.

Societies throughout history have always had to adjust when great technological breakthroughs occurred. It happened with the invention of the printing press, the steam engine, and the electric light. Educators along with all of society must now adjust to present technologically created convulsions. The exciting developments in the application of computers to human learning pose dramatic and vital challenges to teachers, parents, and industry—challenges to which we as a nation must continue to respond, but with more focus and dynamism.

2
THE STRUGGLE FOR CONSTITUTIONAL ORDER

POLAND'S HALF-CENTURY OF TRAGEDY

TAD SZULC

Poland has lived continually with tragedy for nearly one-half of the century—the Nazi tragedy of war and then the Communist tragedy of peace—and this history is vital in understanding the extraordinary Polish events of the 1980s and their continuing impact on communism in a changing world.

First, there was the short but violent war in September 1939 when the vastly superior technology of the German panzer divisions and Stuka dive-bombers smashed Polish resistance (Stalin invaded Poland from the east seventeen days after Hitler's attack to divide the spoils and do away even faster with Poland's army) and thereby triggered World War II.

The Polish defeat on the battlefield was followed by the five-year drama of the German occupation. From the outset, Hitler's master plan was to annihilate Poland as a nation, biologically and spiritually. The Prussians, the Russians, and the Austrians have failed in that endeavor during the 125 years they ruled a partitioned Poland, from the end of the eighteenth century until the collapse of the

Central Powers in 1918—the Poles having remained a cohesive national society, keeping very much alive their national identity, language, culture, and religion—but Hitler believed that the modern technology at the disposal of the Third Reich would be adequate to eradicate the Polish nation.

This master plan provided, after the victory Hitler was certain he would achieve, for the German colonization of Poland. The Poles who survived, or were allowed to survive, would become a pool of slave labor in industry and agriculture. The plan was technologically perfect and detailed; but, of course, it could never be put into effect the way Hitler envisaged it. The fortunes of war created other priorities for the Nazi leadership, even though millions of Poles and others, mainly Jews, perished in concentration camps the Germans had established on Polish territory (as well as elsewhere). These mass murders were executed for the most part with scientific and technological precision.

Hitler's final effort to destroy the Polish nation was the methodic destruction of Warsaw during the uprising late in 1944, his notion presumably being that a nation physically deprived of a capital ceases to be a nation. The Führer obviously had not comprehended that the war was already lost—and his orders to raze Warsaw stemmed from that demented plan he had conceived even before 1939.

It was at the time of the Warsaw uprising that Poland's Nazi and Communist tragedies, in effect, merged into one overwhelming nightmare. Soviet armies had reached the eastern bank of the Vistule River even before the revolt exploded in Warsaw in August 1944, and they simply stopped there. They refused to cross the Vistule and come to the city's rescue despite anguished pleas by the Poles. Stalin had also refused to allow U.S. and British aircraft to land and refuel on Soviet-controlled territory after arms drops for Warsaw's partisans. There is no question that the Soviets were as responsible as the Nazis for the absolute liquidation of Warsaw.

The reason for the Soviet inaction was equally clear. The Warsaw uprising was led by the underground Polish Home Army, known by its Polish initials, AK, under the orders of the exiled non-Communist government in London. The Soviets, in the meantime, had organized their own Polish army under Communist leadership, composed largely of Poles who had been forcibly sent to Siberia from eastern Poland, which the Russians had occupied in 1939.

Since Stalin had all along planned to make Poland part of a postwar satellite region under Communist rule, it was crucial to eliminate the anti-Communist AK forces, the bulk of which were fighting in Warsaw at that stage. The Nazis rendered the Russians a service by eliminating the AK in the process of destroying the capital—with the Soviets watching silently from across the Vistule. This behavior was as cynical of Stalin in 1944 as it was in 1939 when the Soviets signed the nonaggression pact with the Nazis, just before the invasion of Poland. Actually, the commander of a Polish division attached to the Soviet army tried on his own to come to the aid of Warsaw, probably for patriotic reasons, but he was stopped by the Russians and deprived of his command (his memory as a fighter for a liberated Poland was rehabilitated only in the 1980s by the Communist government in Warsaw).

A power vacuum was thus created in Warsaw and the rest of Poland, and Moscow quickly filled it with Polish Communist military and civilian leadership brought from the Soviet Union, first as the interim "Lublin Committee," then as the permanent postwar Communist regime. At the outset, to please the West, a non-Communist faction was tolerated in the cabinet, but it did not last long.

In what people in Poland still regard as an extraordinary outrage against history and national heroism, the Russian and Polish Communists launched a campaign to denigrate the AK as Nazi collaborators, or worse, and portraying the home army, or AL, affiliated with the Communist Polish Workers' Party, as the nation's saviours. In 1939, thousands of Polish officers from the prewar army had been murdered in Katyn, a town in western Russia, and Poles remain convinced that even that far back Stalin had decided that no non-Communist would be left alive to run their country. Now, AK supporters were harassed and imprisoned. This episode is extremely important in judging today's situation in Poland because, even generations later, the humiliation and destruction of the AK have not been forgotten or forgiven. Though the Communists began rehabilitating the AK in the late 1970s, the fate of the home army in the Warsaw uprising and the killing of the officers at Katyn were among major Polish themes evoked when Solidarity was born in 1980 as the greatest movement for rejection of the Communist system in Eastern Europe since the end of the war.

Poland's life as a Communist people's republic started under the most atrocious conditions. The country was devastated by the war, more than any other in Europe, and for all practical purposes its capital no longer existed. The Soviet Union had virtually no resources to spare for Poland's reconstruction, and, as a member of the Soviet bloc, Poland was not allowed by Moscow to accept U.S. aid under the Marshall Plan. Major population shifts occurred when Poland ceded its eastern, mainly agricultural regions to the Soviet Union, and acquired coal-mining and industrialized sections of eastern Germany as part of the redrawing of Europe's map under Moscow's guidance.

Under the circumstances, Poland's model for economic reconstruction and development was to be the "Socialist" one dictated by Moscow, and the nation was launched on what was to be thirty-five years of experimentation with socialism. This period ended, after a fashion, when the free-trade union Solidarity came into being, challenging not only the regime then in power, but also the whole concept of how a modern European nation should be developing. The fact that 10 million Poles, nearly one-third of the population, joined Solidarity demonstrated that the concept of development and management under Communist government was no longer acceptable—certainly not to the new generations—and that it must be replaced by a more rational as well as politically humane philosophy. That the *structure* of Solidarity was smashed by the Communist authorities within two years does not mean a return to the status quo: such a return would be impossible considering the disaster that was the classical Socialist model. Something different had to be invented by the Communists, and they are the first to recognize the "errors of the past" and the reality of the societal shock produced by the events of the 1980s. In this sense, then, Solidarity was a watershed in Polish history—no matter what happens afterward—but it was a phenomenon that flowed logically from the postwar experiences.

These experiences, even within the context of the Socialist model and the total official identification of Poland with the Soviet Union, were intriguingly different from those in other European Communist countries on all levels. Polish character and traditions may explain these differences in a variety of ways—it is a subject for endless historical and sociological debate and analysis—but the Soviets, even under Stalin, had to accept the specificity of Poland.

In the first place, the thirty-five years of socialism were less tragic and spectacular in Poland than elsewhere in Eastern Europe. Hungary, Czechoslovakia, Bulgaria, and Romania lived through a terrifying period in the 1950s, with terror rampant and great show trials of Communist leaders in disgrace, like Laslo Rajk in Budapest and Rudolf Slansky in Prague, and their executions along with so many of their associates. East Germany, though it lived through one episode of anti-Soviet violence in 1953, was —and continues to be—so rigidly and wholly devoted to the Kremlin that even Stalin could not conjure reasons for purges.

Ironically, real terror never materialized in Poland where relatively speaking there was more outspoken political freedom than in the neighboring Soviet satrapies. To be sure, Communist leaders fell from grace, were demoted, and were even imprisoned, but not a single show trial was held there. Nobody was executed. Why? An educated guess is that Moscow realized from the outset that there were no Polish Communist leaders, no matter how faithful to Stalinism in speech and demeanor, who could be counted upon to prepare and carry out trials and other forms of communist purification. Even the strictest critics of Communist regimes in Poland admit that among the successive leaders there really were none who were politically obscene or humanly indecent. No Polish Communist was truly hated as, say, Stalin was hated.

It is possible to suggest that even many of the Moscow-bred Polish Communist leaders came from certain liberal traditions reaching back to the war period and even to the nineteenth century. In their own bizarre ways, some were Polish nationalists, somehow capable of reconciling their patriotism with Moscow's "proletarian internationalism." And it is useful to bear in mind that in Poland there are always contradictions within contradictions and subtleties within subtleties that occasionally help to explain certain political occurrences.

In discussing the Polish character, under communism or not, it is useful to note, of course, the obsessive patriotism that was expressed in bloody anti-Russian uprisings in the nineteenth century, in the music of Frederick Chopin, in the poetry of Adam Mickiewicz, and in the existence of a body of sophisticated literature in the last two centuries that feeds on all facets of national identity. Such traditions, one surmises, do not disappear in the face of the mere thirty-five years of the people's republic experiment—particularly when they are reinforced by the role played in Poland by the Roman Catholic church. This church, one must remember, is part of Polish nationalism for reasons that transcend the fundamental conflict between Catholicism and Marxism. In the nineteenth century, the Polish church was conservative in the social sense, but it was in the vanguard in the centennial battle for the preservation of the Polish identity against foreign rulers who were every bit as conservative.

When the Communists inherited Poland after the war, they arrested the late Stefan Cardinal Wyszynski, harassed the clergy, closed seminaries, and predictably denounced church and religion.

But there was a self-imposed limit in this struggle: the regime never dared to negate in public the religious-nationalist concept that the Black Virgin of Czestochowa is the queen of Poland, and even in the worst Stalinist times the relic with the crown continued to be the object of great veneration.

In time, the cardinal was released, a dialogue developed with the church, and by the time Karol Cardinal Wojtyla of Krakow was elected Pope John Paul II in 1978, the Catholic church and the Marxist state in Poland had reached an extensive modus vivendi. Visiting his homeland both before and after the military coup that dissolved Solidarity in 1981, the Pope was received not only as a head of state (the Vatican), but also as an active participant in the Polish political process. Thus, this strain of the Polish tradition survived the worst of the postwar crises.

In fact, the first postwar political crisis in Poland told as much about the special Polish realities—and the Polish mystique in the practice of politics—as the recent crisis brought on by the Solidarity movement. In October 1956, Communist conservatives confronted liberals over, almost unbelievably, the issue of the freedom of speech by writers and journalists in the context of the Polish economic difficulties, which existed then much as they exist now. There had been riots, and workers were killed by police and army bullets. It was a time when tremendous ferment was sweeping the Communist world in the aftermath of Nikita Khrushchev's "secret" speech ten months earlier before the Soviet Communist party's Central Committee, the speech denouncing the criminal excesses of Joseph Stalin, and the atmosphere in Warsaw was heady with the spreading feeling that accounts should be settled in Poland, too.

Interestingly, however, the incipient revolt in 1956 was not aimed at the destruction of socialism in Poland, but—rather—at the creation of a better and more human form of socialism. This was still a time when a generation of left-wing idealists shared power, or lived close to power, and ideology was very much at stake in this special Polish context with accompanying temptations to go to the furthest extreme. Khrushchev, concerned that the Soviet empire was coming apart in Poland, threatened military intervention. Nevertheless, the rebel Communist leadership placed Wladyslaw Gomulka in power. Gomulka was an old-line party leader who had been under house arrest for some time for the crime of supporting Communist liberals, and Poles of all persuasions thought victory had come with his ascendance.

A few weeks later, the Soviets used tanks to put down an anti-Communist rebellion in Hungary, a movement inspired by the Polish events but aimed at achieving a neutral status for the country (the Poles, for once, had been more careful in terms of their Soviet relationships). Gradually darkness again descended on Eastern Europe. In Warsaw, Gomulka, too, went back to communist orthodoxy. Still, 1956 was a milestone in postwar history—quite possibly the seed from which Solidarity would sprout a generation later.

Today, people in Warsaw say that the Polish population is divided into three basic groups: those who lived through World War II, the 1956 rebellion, and the flowering of Solidarity; those whose political memories begin in 1956; and, finally, those who have come of age politically with the Solidarity experience. These three stages define perfectly Poland's postwar history.

As a great political phenomenon, Solidarity resulted from the egregious failures of Polish socialism in terms of economy, societal conditions, and the relationship between the regime and the population. By and large, however, its goal was not to replace socialism with capitalism (as Moscow propaganda claims), but to mold a form of intelligent Polish socialism—or Polish social democracy with Sweden as a model—under which the human and material resources of the nation could be put to best use.

Historically, Solidarity's roots go to the immediate postwar period of certain Socialist idealism, to the ferment of 1956, and to the conflict between the government and the nation that reached a point of immense gravity when security forces shot and killed workers in Gdansk's shipyards protesting rises in food prices, just before Christmas 1970. It was Gomulka who ordered this action, and this led to his overthrow by his fellow Communist leaders, the second time the party had to bow to public opinion—an event never matched elsewhere in the Soviet empire.

Between 1970 and 1980, Polish intellectuals and workers were able for the first time to find common ground in joint political action. The alliance took shape in 1976 when food riots again erupted in the country and culminated in Solidarity's birth. Lech Walesa's top advisers were the intellectuals drawn from the growing dissident movement in Poland, the dissidents who put together an underground press and a clandestine university.

What made this alliance possible—and this is perhaps the key factor in present-day Polish developments—was the considerable degree of education attained in postwar Poland. Ironically, education of good quality was one of the few achievements of Polish socialism. But when the sons of the workers and the peasants became educated by the regime, they began to think, ask questions, criticize, and ultimately reach a state of total alienation from the system with its rampant inefficiency, cynicism, and corruption.

For these reasons, the stage was set for the emergence of Solidarity as both a labor and political movement when conflicts over work conditions led to strikes in Gdansk and elsewhere in July and August 1980. The Communist party found itself again on the defensive, working out a pact with Solidarity workers and firing Edward Gierek, the man who had replaced Gomulka after the bloodshed ten years earlier. For the third time, public opinion in this Communist country forced a change in leadership.

Ample studies exist concerning the nature and extent of economic mismanagement by the Polish Communist party that led to the 1980 crisis. It is worthwhile to note that, in a way, greed for high technology helped to aggravate the economic situation in Poland. Anxious to turn Poland into an advanced industrial state capable of earning foreign currency through the export of manufactured goods, the Gierek regime had gone more than $15 billion into debt to Western bankers to acquire this technology.

It was presumably commendable for Poland to seek modernization (and the West was the only source of technology), but the regime's disastrous central planning system could not digest it. Raw materials could not be supplied on time or in adequate volume to the new plants; there were no quality-control systems; financial resources' allocations were senseless; and, in the end, billions of dollars of Western technology were being wasted as equipment either stood idle or deteriorated.

Just as critically, the regime never could solve Poland's farm production problem. Though from the beginning that special Polish character of socialism had saved the country from land collectivization—most of the land is in private hands in small holdings and cooperatives—the Socialist experiment failed utterly in making agriculture function in terms of organizing markets, providing fertilizer, and, in general, providing farmers with the required incentive to produce. Billions of dollars were spent annually on food imports.

Solidarity's stated goal was to rationalize the economy. But Poland was never given a chance. Eighteen months were spent in disputes between the regime and Solidarity (while the Communist party was rotting away as an instrument of government) and in growing Soviet threats that the liquidation of socialism would not be tolerated in Poland by the Socialist brethren.

On December 13, 1981, the military moved, taking over the management of Polish affairs. Nearly ten thousand Solidarity militants were interned as the army and the security police swept the country in a superbly prepared operation. A military council headed by General Wojciech Jaruzelski, who also was prime minister, assumed the tasks of administration. Martial law was declared.

Curiously, it was technology that, as never before in a political situation, was of immense importance both in the birth and the death of Solidarity. From its creation, the free union maintained contact with its militants in industrial plants, mines, shipyards, and farms through an unlimited use of telex and telephone facilities. Modern communications made it possible for Solidarity to plan its moves, tactics, and strategy in a way that would have been impossible under any dictatorship. In Poland, however, even the Communist dictatorship in 1980 and 1981 was so full of contradictions that everything seemed—and often was—feasible.

When the generals launched their coup d'état, their first step was to paralyze all telex communications in Poland and to suspend telephone service in the entire country. Unable to communicate, Solidarity's militants were defenseless. But the coup also showed how dependent a modern society is on such routine technology as telephones. During the six weeks during which the telephone system simply did not exist, the Polish society became almost motionless in terms of everything from business to social and family relations. Only the military and the police had instant communications and thus could monitor every move in the country. State radio and television told the nation what was occurring, and what people were—or were not—allowed to do. For months, for example, they could not travel abroad because all the transportation links with foreign countries were severed. Travel within the country was banned for weeks simply by stopping gasoline sales and halting air and surface public transportation.

No modern society can endure such restrictions for an extended period, and the Polish generals lifted them when they felt the situation was under control. They demonstrated, however, that—at least for a time—a challenge to a dictatorial regime could be defused simply by depriving a society of basic technology and, without bloodshed, of a Polish way of doing things.

Polish problems are being handled (if not necessarily resolved) in that Polish way, a way that would be unthinkable in other Communist countries. The martial law has been lifted, but the regime knows it cannot truly crush Solidarity and its spirit, and therefore it is forced to deal—almost negotiate—with the opposition.

Lech Walesa, Solidarity's chief, was released from prison during 1983, but the government has been unable to make him a "nonperson" despite great efforts. He goes around criticizing the regime, giving interviews to foreign journalists (who are allowed to interview him and to transmit their material abroad), and his fame reached a new climax with the award of the Nobel Peace Prize. The prize was given because nonviolence was Solidarity's fundamental principle. There are occasional riots, and Western television is free to broadcast images of Polish riot squads beating up demonstrators. It is political surrealism and Communist surrealism. Above all, it is Poland, which is something very special in our age of high technology and regimentation. It is a country where ancient human values still define the life of the new generations.

COERCIVE RULE IN SOUTH AFRICA

GWENDOLEN M. CARTER

Our major task is to ensure that a white nation will prevail here. Every nation has the inalienable right to safeguard that which it has built for itself and for posterity. This then is our task . . . but we know that this cannot be done by suppressing those entrusted to our care; neither can they be denied the opportunity to develop fully. This is a lesson that history has taught us, and which we know only too well. It is disgraceful that the outside world associates the concept of Separate Development with oppression.

Prime Minister H. F. Verwoerd
September 3, 1963

I am surprised at the conditions that the government wants to impose on me. I am not a violent man. My colleagues and I wrote in 1952 to [Prime Minister] Malan asking for a round table conference to find a solution to the problems of our country, but that was ignored. When Strijdom was in power, we made the same offer. Again it was ignored. When Verwoerd was in power we asked for a national convention for all the people in South Africa to decide on their future. This, too, was in vain.

It was only then when all other forms of resistance were no longer open to us that we turned to armed struggle. Let Botha show that he is different to Malan, Strijdom and Verwoerd. Let him renounce violence. Let him say that he will dismantle apartheid. Let him unban the people's organisation [sic], the African National Congress. Let him free all who have been imprisoned, banished or exiled for their opposition to apartheid. Let him guarantee free political activity so that people may decide who will govern them.

I cherish my own freedom dearly, but I care even more for your freedom.

Only free men can negotiate.

I cannot and will not give any undertaking at a time when I and you, the people, are not free.

Your freedom and mine cannot be separated. I will return.

> Nelson Mandela's response to
> an offer of release by
> President P. W. Botha if
> Mandela would foreswear
> violence, as read by his
> daughter, Zinzi Mandela, to a mass
> rally in Soweto on February 10,
> 1985

South Africa's white minority has long operated a smoothly running parliamentary system whose members are selected in regularly held elections, following accepted procedures. The country's courts are constantly in session and, technically, they are color blind. Superficially, the democratic processes and a complementary system of justice appear to be operating. An examination of the laws administered, however, reveals that South African institutions underwrite the discriminatory racial system commonly known as apartheid or "separate development." They provide white administrators with broad grants of power to determine where members of other racial groups may live and when they may legally enter white areas, sell their labor, or take up domicile. Enforcing these and many other restrictions, particularly on the African majority, is a host of penal provisions at the disposal of the police, backed up, if necessary, by the army.

Control over the allocation of space and guarantees of a steady supply of cheap labor have long been crucial to the well-being and prosperity of the white minority. As far back as the nineteenth century, white settler and colonial governments developed native policies that gave them economic and political control of the indigenous population. After Union in 1910, however, efforts to evolve a uniform African policy were complicated by the sharp divisions between mine owners and farmers. The mine owners wanted subsistence agriculture in the African reserves to supplement the low wages they paid in mines, but the farmers wanted as much land and African labor for themselves as possible.

The Native Land Act in 1913 designated certain areas as African reserves but prohibited Africans from buying or independently occupying land outside the 7 percent of the country's area allocated to them, most of it in Natal and the Eastern Cape. Thousands of relatively prosperous African sharecroppers and cash tenants, as well as squatters, were pushed off the land and became semi-proletarianized. Barely enough land was left to Africans to provide a subsistence base for the migrant workers at the mines. Although promised more land in the Hertzog-Smuts "settlement" of 1936, the total land possessed by Africans today is still less than the 13.7 percent envisaged then. Moreover, through the 1936 arrangement, male Cape Africans lost their historic right to vote on the common roll for candidates for Parliament that only they possessed.

The Afrikaner Nationalist electoral victory in 1948 led to new and far-reaching means to implement the party's cherished policies of racial separation. By that time, the impact of World War II had caused major population changes both on the farms and in the urban areas; the 1951 census disclosed that Africans slightly outnumbered whites, 2.3 million to 2.1 million. The rapidly changing character of industrial development in South Africa, from its heavy dependence on relatively unskilled labor to an increasing demand for skilled labor, called for new policies.

The response to the postwar situation by the new government was swift and drastic. Influx-control regulations were rigidly enforced against African men and women. These restrictions were based mainly on older legislation, in particular the Natives (Urban Areas) Act of 1923, which turned all towns into "proclaimed areas" in which no African could remain legally for more than seventy-two hours unless he or she had Labour Bureau approval as migrant labor or met so-called Section 10 provisions. These qualifications were and remain: birth in the area; fifteen years of lawful residence; service with the same employer for ten continuous years; or a relationship as wife, son, or unmarried daughter of someone fulfilling those conditions. Coupled with the requirement that all male Africans (and subsequently also African women) carry a pass, the hated badge of servitude, these provisions led to massive exclusions of large numbers of previously urban African residents: 456,000 from twenty-three towns between 1956 and 1963.

In addition, the Resettlement of Natives Act of 1954 was used to force some sixty thousand Africans from the so-called Western Areas to a new section farther outside Johannesburg. African freehold rights in certain urban areas also came under attack and, in a process that also still continues, were abolished in three suburbs of Pretoria that were turned over to white occupancy and ownership.

It has not only been Africans who have suffered resettlement since the Afrikaner Nationalist government took office. The Group Areas Act of 1950, cornerstone of apartheid, zoned all residential areas for exclusive occupancy or ownership by particular racial groups: white, Colored (mixed race), Indian, or African. The Colored, who today form the majority population in the Western Cape, and the Indians, whose numbers are more or less equivalent to those of the whites in and around Durban, have suffered severely through rezoning.

Mass removals and population relocation remain constant features of contemporary South Africa. Their dimensions during the period from 1960 to 1982 have been meticulously documented through a large-scale voluntary research effort known as the Surplus Peoples Project. Started in 1980, its results have been published, beginning in January 1983, in five volumes under the title *Forced Removals in South Africa*. The details provided by these studies reveal that more than 3.5 million people have been removed, often by force, and resettled during the twelve-year period. Three-quarters to four-fifths of them have been Africans, and the rest, Colored or

Indians. The project estimated that 2 million more members of these three groups were threatened with removal in the near future.

The Colored, whose primary right to jobs in the Western Cape was long protected by a policy of preference, suffered the loss of their historic District 6, whose proximity to Cape Town's business section ultimately sealed its fate. Although the Colored with adequate resources can find private housing in the new city built at Mitchell Plains on the far side of Cape Town, the poor in that community must share with Africans the windswept Cape Flats, which are far from the kind of jobs they can hope to secure. Unprecendented rioting by the Colored in 1976 and again in 1980 indicated their frustration at what has been happening to them.

Residential segregation of Indians in Durban is just as unpopular. Although the development of three new living areas on the edges of town—Chatworth, Phoenix, and Newlands West—has reduced if not eliminated removals under the Group Areas Act, middle-class Indians resent the white domination of housing in the city's center as well as in Natal. For low-income Indians, the housing patterns extending over a twenty-year period have only led, according to a recent analysis, to "impoverishment and resentment."

The major impact of forced resettlement has fallen, as can be expected, on the Africans. It is intimately correlated with the evolution of the "homeland," Bantustan, or national states policy, the ultimate expression and essential feature of separate development. In 1959, the Promotion of Bantu Self-Government Act recognized eight "black national units" formed out of scattered reserves. Each had a distinctive ethnic character. Eight years before, the Bantu Authorities Act has replaced the local government administrative system in the reserves with what were considered more appropriate tribal, regional, and territorial authorities. Chiefs were given greater powers, the former elective aspects of administration were reduced, and overall ultimate white control was ensured.

In the same period, Africans were effectively cut off from their previous links to the country's lawmaking system. The national

Natives Representatives Council, established in 1936 as an organ for consultation with the government, was abolished in 1951. In 1959, the government abolished the indirect representation of Africans in Parliament through specially chosen whites, which itself had been intended as a substitute for the Cape Africans' 1936 loss of their franchise on the common roll. Despite much greater opposition by liberal whites, the Colored were removed from the common voting roll in 1956, and they lost their indirect representation by selected whites in 1968.

The African "homelands," presently numbering ten and primarily situated on the periphery of South Africa, are in the government's view the appropriate representative entities responsible for the African majority. Africans domiciled in or ethnically linked to four—Transkei, Bophuthatswana, Venda, and Ciskei—have accepted an independence that no other state recognizes, in return for the loss of their South African citizenship. A fifth "homeland," KwaNdebele, is expected to accept independence soon. Its proximity to Pretoria makes possible a daily commute by fast train to jobs in the city, considered by the government to be a particularly desirable way of securing labor without increasing the number of urban Africans.

Since the early 1960s, the government's program of enforced African resettlement in the "homelands" has pressed ahead, sometimes by persuasion, often by coercion. Africans have been forced out of towns, cities, and farming areas from one end of the country to the other. Though the majority have been unskilled or semi-skilled workers, the dispossessed have also included those whose skills are no longer needed. As a result, the proportion of the total African population living in the "homelands" had risen from 39.5 percent in 1960 to 54 percent in 1980. And still the flow continues.

High on the list of those forced to leave their homes are residents of African communities that are commonly known as "black spots," settlements completely surrounded by white-owned or white-occupied land. Many of these African communities have long histories. One of the few whose fate received the publicity that has generally been lacking elsewhere was Driefontein in the Transvaal. Driefontein had been established one year prior to the Natives Land Act in 1913, having been bought the year before on behalf of the Native Farmers' Association of Africa, Ltd., by Pixley ka Isaka Seme, a founder of the African National Congress and its president from 1930 to 1937. Driefontein was, therefore, on freehold land. Its five thousand inhabitants built productive farms, in addition to wells, shops, schools, churches, and sturdy houses. When the government painted numbers on the buildings, a signal of impending resettlement, the inhabitants joked about it at first. When the numbers were painted on gravestones, the residents were outraged. The police came on April 2, 1983, to accelerate the move. Saul Mkhize, a migrant worker who had written to Prime Minister Botha to protest the move, argued with them. Impatient, the young white policeman in charge returned to his car, took out his gun, and shot and killed Mkhize. As word spread, many came to his funeral to protest as much as to mourn, but the removal went on nevertheless.

The Colored and the Indians, by contrast, have accepted the government's policy of African separateness even though the policy is underwritten by a fearsome array of coercive legislation. In 1952–53, Africans staged a nationwide passive resistance campaign against "unjust laws." In 1955, a massive multiracial Congress of the People affirmed in the Freedom Charter "that South Africa belongs to all who live in it, black and white." The government response was a drawn-out treason trial in 1955 of 156 African, Colored, Indian, and white leaders of nationalist and protest movements, all of whom were ultimately acquitted by 1961. In the meantime, however, a peaceful demonstration against the pass laws had led to the shooting of unarmed Africans at Sharpeville on March 21, 1960, killing 72 and wounding more than 150 others. The national and international reactions to the massacre led to the proclamation of a state of emergency, the passage of the Unlawful Organizations Act that same year, and its use to ban both the African

National Congress, whose multiracial membership had long been in the forefront of the struggle for African rights, and the Pan-Africanist Congress.

White South Africans are privileged persons in comparison with those in other racial categories, but they too may be subject to surveillance and harsh penalties for participating in protest movements that the government labels subversive. The executive has nearly unlimited discretion by virtue of powers granted under the Suppression of Communism Act of 1950, the Internal Security Act of 1970, and other subsequent legislation. The 1950 act not only dissolved the Communist party but also empowered the state president to declare any other organization unlawful by simple proclamation, without either giving it notice or the opportunity to testify in its own defense. These provisions were reaffirmed in the Unlawful Organizations Act of 1960.

Once an organization has been declared unlawful, there can be far-reaching penalties for anyone shown to be or believed to be a member. One penalty is banning, a practice that restricts the person to a particular district and to meeting with only one other person at a time. It may also require the person to report regularly—sometimes daily—to the local police station. An extreme form of banning restricts a person to house arrest. The first person to suffer this extreme restriction was Helen Joseph, a white woman who had been among the 156 persons in the 1955 treason trial. She had also been one of the leaders of the massive multiracial, though unsuccessful, protest on August 9, 1956, by twenty thousand women against forcing African women to carry passes.

Detention without trial is also a feature of South African security legislation. In 1963, the General Laws Amendment Act authorized the interrogation of persons held in solidarity confinement for up to ninety days. Two years later, detention for 180 days to answer questions from the authorities was made a permanent part of the criminal procedure. In 1967, the Terrorism Act provided for indefinite detention without trial.

Although there are major difficulties in determining who is being detained and where, the Detainees' Parents' Support Committee (DPSA), an informal association of parents and relatives of detainees, has collected a great deal of evidence to support allegations that, since 1963, 52 persons have died in detention and 191 persons were being held in detention without access to legal advice or to the courts during 1982. If the "homelands" are taken into account, the number of detainees was 800 in 1981, 300 in 1982, and 127 in the first half of 1983. The deaths in detention of the founder of the Black Consciousness Movement, Steven Biko, on September 12, 1977, and of Neil Aggett, a white physician who worked with a black trade union, on February 5, 1982, are among the few on which detailed information has been secured of what goes on in an otherwise impenetrable system.

On June 30, 1983, the banning orders for the sixty-five persons then under the restriction lapsed in terms of Section 73 (12) of the revised Internal Security Act of a year earlier, but banning was immediately reimposed on ten of them, including Winnie Mandela, a prominent nationalist figure in her own right and the wife of the leader of the African National Congress, Nelson Mandela, who has long been imprisoned for life. Mrs. Mandela has also suffered banishment to Brandford, a small town in the Orange Free State. Another prominent person, Dr. Beyers Naude, a distinguished Afrikaans clergyman who has long maintained his stand against apartheid restrictions, was banned again in October 1982 but freed from restrictions in 1984. He succeeded Bishop Desmond Tutu as director of the South African Council of Churches after the latter was awarded the Nobel Prize and became bishop of Johannesburg.

Although there was a general sense of relief that banning restrictions were removed from many who had long suffered under them, the government's power to impose banning at will remains intact. A new list drawn up by the director of security legislation names individuals who cannot be quoted in South

Africa either during their lifetime or thereafter—a list with 134 names.

Persons subject to this "listing" were originally the officers, members, or suspected supporters of groups declared by the government to be unlawful. Under Section 10 of the Internal Security Act, they now include persons of all races convicted after June 1982 of government-defined communism, terrorism, or sedition. They were held by the court to include Barbara Hogan, whose acknowledged commitment to the African National Congress led to a ten-year sentence of solitary confinement for treason, despite the fact that she had not even participated in any demonstrations on behalf of the congress. Section 10 also covers "printing, publishing or disseminating" any material in contravention of any government regulation, thereby enlarging the already considerable anxieties and potential restrictions under which the South African press and other organizations must operate.

On November 3, 1983, white voters endorsed by a substantial majority a new constitution, which for the first time in the country's history established a tripartite Parliament in which representatives of the 3 million Colored and 875,000 Indians each have their own chamber, as the representatives of the 20.6 million whites have long enjoyed. The 23 million blacks are still excluded from representation. Each of the enfranchised groups is responsible for legislation affecting its own exclusive affairs. National legislation, like the Group Areas Act and the budget, however, is voted on jointly by the representatives in all three houses, among whom the white house commands a decisive majority. The new constitution also provides for a president, elected for five years by an electoral college in which whites have a majority. Combining the powers of the old offices of prime minister and state president, P. W. Botha, president under the new constitution, became the most powerful individual in the country's history.

All three racial groups involved under the new constitution had been sharply divided in their reactions to it. The inclusion of Colored and Indians in Parliament had been bitterly opposed by right-wing Afrikaner Nationalists. The explicit exclusion of Africans, the country's majority population, from any role in the new constitution led to sharp protests from every racial group. It also led to strikingly low participation by Colored and Indian registered voters for their candidates for Parliament, 30 percent of those eligible among the former and 20 percent of the latter. Since registration among both groups had also been very low, the number of Colored and Indians who participated in the election represented an even smaller percentage of potential voters from the groups.

Among the urbanized members of the approximately 23 million Africans, the exclusion from the new constitution and the imposition on the townships of a third tier of local administration led to intense bitterness, unrest, country-wide school boycotts, and sporadic violence, particularly against those considered collaborators. The bitterness and violence increased when the government sent in troops and police to establish order.

The character of the new constitution was also one of the factors that led to the formation of two new organizations dedicated to fundamental change in South Africa. The largest of these organizations, the United Democratic Front (UDF), was organized formally on August 20–21, 1983. A locally based front for some affiliated groups including trade unions, churches, and community organizations, it has a membership of more than a million people of all races. Although the names of some of its patrons indicated a kinship with the banned African National Congress and the Freedom Charter's declaration that "South Africa belongs to all its people, black and white," the UDF has been careful to avoid any explicit relationship. Nonetheless, in February 1985, the government imprisoned sixteen of its leaders and charged them with treason. Other UDF figures are being held for questioning. The government has also threatened to ban UDF activities and, at the end of March 1985, did so along with programs of twenty-eight other organizations for a period of three months.

The second major group, the National Front, or Forum, was launched on June 11–12, 1983, by two hundred black organizations, including the trade unions. The Front has pointedly omitted any mention of whites in the struggle for a nonracial South Africa and specified "racial capitalism" as its major goal. Its most vocal member, AZAPO (Azanian People's Organization), demonstrated noisily during Senator Edward M. Kennedy's visit to South Africa in January 1985.

The most promising development in South Africa has been the growth and stability of African trade unions. Legalized in 1979, they have expanded into several confederations. The most prominent is the Federation of South African Trade Unions, with more than one hundred thousand members, affiliates in the automobile, steel, and textile industries, and almost all its members African and Colored. In addition, there are the Council of Unions of South Africa, a federation of nine all-African trade unions with more than fifty thousand workers, the National Union of Mineworkers, and the South African Allied Workers Union.

A planned two-day protest strike by the black trade unions in fall 1984, aimed at the new constitution, provided impressive evidence of discipline and had a strong impact. The government-owned SASOL (oil from coal) dismissed all six thousand African workers in retaliation for the strike but subsequently rehired a substantial number of those with special skills. Despite the initial reaction at SASOL to the strike, African trade unions are one area where the government has been somewhat restrained in using its coercive power.

In opening the first working session of the new tricameral Parliament, in January 1985, President Botha made an impressive speech in which he spoke of a future cooperative coexistence in South Africa, in which "there is no domination of one population group over another" and in which there is "self determination for each group over its own affairs and joint responsibility for, and cooperation in, common interests," a striking and potentially far-reaching goal. In addition, he spoke of cooperation on matters of common interest within the same overall framework. He declared that the government would look into granting full property rights to Africans in certain urban areas in South Africa as well as in the so-called self-governing states and would consider a more satisfactory arrangement for the resettlement of communities along with restrictions on influx control. Most surprising was his overture to Nelson Mandela, the long-imprisoned leader of the African National Congress, the historic standardbearer of African nationalism. The offer of release from prison if Mandela would renounce violence was met, not surprisingly, by Mandela's refusal, as stated at the beginning of this chapter, then withdrawn.

Unfortunately, what had seemed a more promising attitude by the government was seriously clouded by the police killings during their January 1985 raid on the shantytown known as Crossroads outside Cape Town, where some fifty to one hundred thousand Africans have been living precariously for the last decade. Subsequently, national and international reactions to the violence led to an agreement that its inhabitants will not be forced to move to the more remote sand dunes of Khayelitsha. Further brutal police action against peaceful demonstrations, however, and, most disturbing of all, against massive funeral processions, as at Uitenhage on the twenty-fifth anniversary of the Sharpeville massacre, suggests that some of the worst excesses may be due at least in part to inadequate control over the police. A hunkering-down in the face of mounting foreign criticism and economic sanctions has further burst the promise that had risen like a balloon from Botha's speech.

The South African government possesses virtually unlimited power to try to shape its people's lives and livelihoods to fit the overall pattern of racial segregation and conformist behavior that is embodied in so many of the country's laws and regulations. It also has the power, should it choose to use it, to improve the condition of all its people, of all races. South Africa's white military leaders have described the implicit conflict within the country as 80 percent political and only 20 percent military. The chief military commander said in 1983 that the government must "win the hearts and minds of our indigeneous people." So far, there is little evidence that the new constitution or any other government initiative has yet served to build an enhanced sense of unity within the country. Should the government use its vast power not for coercion, however, but to answer the manifold needs of all its people—African, Colored, Indian, as well as white—South Africa might at last move toward internal stability and relative harmony.

THE RISE AND FALL OF SPANISH ABSOLUTISM

CHARLES F. GALLAGHER

Human Bondage, in the words of Spinoza, is the price of Human Freedom. The advantages of the first state (and Human Bondage has many and substantial advantages) are incompatible with those of the second. We must be content to pay, and indefinitely to go on paying, the irreducible price of the goods we have chosen.
Aldous Huxley, Beyond the Mexique Bay

If George Orwell, who was an outspoken opponent of dogmatism and blind ideology, could return in 1984 to the Spain he reported from and fought in during the civil war of 1936–39, he would find changes so far reaching that his sometimes faltering faith in democratic socialism might well be rekindled. It would seem a miracle to someone who had become disillusioned by the brutalities of both sides, and by the lies of opposing governments, rabble-rousers, and reporters, to see decades later—as he often must have wished to see in the immediate aftermath—that neither brand of despotism (and both sides fitted that description as the war progressed) won in the long run.

Orwell admitted, in *Homage to Catalonia,* that he knew little of the background of the vicious rivalries that led to his wounding and subsequent flight from the country in 1937. But he would now see that what he thought he was upholding when he went to "the defense of civilization against a maniacal outbreak by an army of Colonel Blimps in the pay of Hitler," but which he came to realize was far more complex than that, has in fact emerged as an amazingly harmonious resolution of that complexity—at least as harmonious as can be conceived in an imperfect political world, and more than could ever have been imagined in the thick of the fighting in which he took part.

For the "transition" in contemporary Spain is not simply a change from dictatorship to democracy, as is usually thought, but the "transformation" of a society from subjection to contending absolutisms, theological and secular, reactionary and revolutionary, to a mutually tolerant society of a dimension never before attained in Spanish history. This transformation has required a major shift in fundamental attitudes, the magnitude of which is hard to overstress. It involves an escape from "Romance" politics, which exist as surely as do Romance languages.

The main tenets of Romance politico-religious ideology can be simply stated. They rest on twin pillars of absolutism and oligarchy. One group—our group—possesses the truth and the whole truth, and no outside ideas can form part of that truth. Moreover, the social pie is inelastic: what is beneficial to one group is necessarily detrimental to the others. It is a doctrine of "no common good" and, as a corollary, it attempts to stretch the static social pie, which is conceived of as part of a natural order. The interpenetration of political and religious absolutism is an essential part of this system—just as political and religious pluralism have tended to go hand in hand—and thus any effort to subvert the hierarchical view of life is ultimately viewed not simply as political dissent but as religious heresy.

Because there is no common good, individuals do not feel bound by impersonal loyalties to those beyond their nearest horizon, and they do not accept the state as the final arbiter of the social compact. This narrowness of social vision in turn leads to an autocratic personalism at all behavioral levels, whether the action is concerned with the maintenance of the status quo or is directed toward social change.

Since the state is not fully recognized as an impersonal referee in human affairs but is considered rather as a co-vicar on earth of higher values, it has to compete with a number of social institutions that are subsidiary in modern secular societies. The foremost of these is the church, with which the state nominally cooperates in keeping a divinely ordained order but with which it may find itself in subtle forms of conflict.

The downgrading of the legitimate functions of the state and the pressures of competing institutions result in lessened obedience to generalized legal sanctions, which often are ineffective or unheeded, and consequently in a laxness in their enforcement in areas felt to be of lesser importance but with sporadically forceful intervention in matters suddenly thought urgent. The rule of a generalized, impersonal legal system accepted by all is vitiated, and the state, having less authority, acts in unpredictable, intermittent outbursts of force.

The failure of impersonal social norms to take root has another consequence in Romance politico-religious life. As Gino Germani pointed out in discussing the retention of primary ties and their fusion with modern traits in modernized political systems, there is a "frequent intrusion of expressive behavior in non-primary relationships in advanced Latin societies." Latin political life is intensely personal, highly affective and emotional, and segmented by the existence of multiple, rival social institutions—all this fragmented corpus, however, functioning on a level subordinate to the eternal order sanctified by the church and expressed by the state in the doctrine of "two swords."

There are several variants on the Latin theme, given the historical experience of each Romance country: Italy, Spain, and Portugal, as well as the offshoots of the latter two in Ibero-America. The purest form, however, and the longest-lasting one, from the Middle Ages until 1975, has certainly been Spain.

George Orwell stumbled onto Spain at a time when the traditional system, which had recently come under sustained attack by modernizing forces in Spanish society during the Second Republic (1931–36), was violently counterattacking. Like anyone else he could appreciate that, but what he did not understand was that this struggle was the culmination of a centuries-long process in which Spanish history had become completely warped.

The central theme of Spanish history was shaped as early as a thousand years ago, in response to the Muslim conquest that left large areas of the Iberian Peninsula occupied for seven centuries. The pursuit of religious unity was the ultimate ideal, with a higher priority than political or cultural unity, although both would later be subsumed under the banner of an integral realm of faith. This drive was succinctly described by Salvador de Madariaga in *Spain: A Modern History:*

Spain was thrust on the world stage by an impulse directed toward religious unity. Such an impulse was to dominate all her policy at home, in Europe and overseas. At home it explains the Inquisition, the decay of the university, the drying up of sources of intellectual leadership in her middle classes, the impoverishment of her civil service, and in the end, the lamentable weakness of the state.

The movement toward this goal, unconscious at first but by the fifteenth century carefully orchestrated, meant the gradual creation of a closed society in which full membership was accorded only to those of one religious persuasion, and later only to those who proved the purity of their religious ancestry in hereditary terms.

The price of the ideal was high, for it also meant the rejection of a more open commonwealth that could have included the large body of Muslim Spaniards, the Spanish Jews, and in the sixteenth century the bearers of the intellectual ferment of the Reformation and the scientific revolution that stemmed from it. Instead the Muslims, who were overwhelmingly of Spanish and not foreign blood, were reconverted by force and confined in castelike occupations in an operation begun in 1502 and concluded by 1610, when the last of them were expelled from Spanish soil. A similar fate befell the Jews, many more of whom converted than did the Muslims, but to little avail, for their banishment came even earlier, in 1492. It is worth recalling that from those dates until 1976 there existed in Spain not one mosque or synagogue, and that until 1966 no non-Catholic Christian religious ceremony could be publicly celebrated. One of the prerequisities of a closed system was thereby established: unanimity of belief protected from internal deviation and external contamination.

This condition of cloistered certainty was not achieved without difficulties. It had to overcome the subversive potential of the mixed, though separate, cultures. Toledo's School of Translators and the inquisitive intellectual atmosphere generated by it, the dangers of the warm cultural synthesis in medieval Seville, and the influence of the Mozárabes (Arabized Spanish Christians) and the Mudéjares (Spanish Muslims living in areas retaken by the Christians), both of which lived in large numbers and for long periods in mutual tolerance. To explain this, a leading Spanish historian has written:

The appearance of the ideal of a Crusade (which seems to me a good basis for interpretation and one which has been verified) seems to conflict with the subsequent tendency of Christians, Moors, and Jews to achieve a harmonious accord within a common social and intellectual abode. The contradiction does exist; the explanation is that the Christian-Islamic integration was an urban event, while antagonism between Christians and converted Muslims (Moriscos) was a rural phenomenon. Royalty oscillated between the two camps, protecting now one and then the other, until the decision of the Catholic Monarchs—a decision that is dramatic from so many points of view. [The Catholic monarchs, Ferdinand and Isabella, ordered the expulsion of Jews in 1492, forcing them to convert or emigrate. In 1502 they decreed the expulsion of all Muslims in the former Kingdom of Granada who did not convert (in violation of the agreement made when that last Muslim state surrendered in 1492). In 1525 this decree was extended to the Kingdom of Aragon.] (Jaime Vicens Vives, *Aproximacion a la Historia de Espana*)

The vital role played by the School of Translators in stimulating thought and science in Oxford, Bologna, and Paris in the thirteenth century is in complete contrast to the fact that, as Spanish historians point out, its output was exported to Europe without leaving any trade in Castile. The reason lies in the evolving nature of Christian Spain as it moved from its first self-perceptions around A.D. 1000 to the definitive enunciation of policy on the unity of the faith laid down by 1500.

Castile began as a frontier realm ripe with opportunity, in which booty, land, and privileges rewarded the successful fighter against infidels, usually thought of a heretics. Here a class of small, freehold proprietors and minor nobles (*hidalgos*) grew up, imbued with a spirit of toughness, egalitarianism, and religious chauvinism, all of which came to form an essential part of the core of Hispanic life.

After the conquest of Toledo in 1085, however, the evident superiority of urban Muslim civilization produced a period of awed tolerance, permitting the former Muslim capital to serve as a transfer point of Judeo-Arabic learning to the rest of Europe. But to the rough-hewn, rural Castilian society of shepherds and peasant-warriors, the city remained an alien flower and in the end it failed to take root in the kingdom, whose most typical towns were and still are austere mountain citadels like Avila, Segovia, and Burgos. After the death of Alfonso X in 1284, the court, rustic and ill at ease there, left to migrate periodically, like the flocks of its pastors, from town to town on the meseta of Old Castile. The knightly elite of this land were uninterested in and incapable of understanding the subtleties of Greek philosophy or the complexities of mathematics and grammar, so they shut these disciplines out of their narrow world and unconcernedly passed them on to the countries beyond the Pyrenees.

Social and demographic factors were changing during the thirteenth and fourteenth centuries, however, as the Reconquest moved south into Extremadura and Andalucia. Previously, fighter-settlers were occupying sparsely inhabited lands in the north, but in southern Spain the crusade was given over to recently founded religio-military orders: the Knights of Calatrava, of Santiago, and of Ancantara, among others, who founded large estates on which conquered Muslim peasants (or occasionally demobilized Christian foot soldiers) came to occupy positions as hired hands or renters. Thus the latifundia system was born and became a model to be repeated in the conquest of the New World, where the same conditions prevailed of a conquered race that could be harshly dealt with because it lay outside the sphere of divine grace.

With the emergence of the knightly orders, the concept of the sword as a constant servant of religion was enhanced and linked to an idea of honor that disdained commerce and manual labor. By 1300, Muslims and Jews made up a sizable part of the urban population of both Castile (now including Andalucia) and Aragon. The Muslims soon dominated the artisanal and skilled trades sectors, and the Jews took charge of commerce and banking. Religious divisions were in this way complemented by a new separation of social classes, in which a parasitical aristocracy dedicated to war and faith looked askance at heretical groups that it associated with despised economic activities. The egalitarianism of Old Castile was increasingly replaced by a hierarchical mold, in which the military and the church militant jointly predominated. Thus the important evolutionary role played by merchant guilds in northern Europe, of laying the foundations for free municipal institutions, was lacking in Spain, where, just as in Islamic society, this stratum was composed of minority groups who were outside the sacral entity and not full citizens.

By the early fifteenth century, anti-Jewish and anti-Muslim decrees were enacted. Distinctive clothing was prescribed, specific occupations were prohibited, and unchangeable domiciles assigned. To avoid these vexations, many converted, so many in fact that the converts became more suspect than those who refused to apostatize, so that the main line of division became that distinguishing "old Christians" from the *conversos*. Certificates of "blood purity" were soon required for full admission to the benefits of society (as in 1418 at the University of Salamanca), the rights of the recently converted were increasingly limited, and their testimony could not be accepted fully in court. The Vatican itself raised its voice against such practices, proclaiming that "all Catholics form one body with Christ," but without success.

By the end of the fifteenth century the Catholic monarchs, Ferdinand and Isabella, had forged a national entity that needed a national ideology. It was to be based on religious unity and purity and expressed in a national church that, although fully a part of the Roman Catholic Church, often acted apart from it. Again Madariaga has best summarized the essence of the rule of the *reyes catolicos:*

Under their common rule the Spanish anarchy became a state and the Spanish state became a church. Not, be it understood, The Church; least of all, the Roman Church. The expulsion of the Jews was not a Roman but a Spanish idea. The Inquisition was conceived and founded as a department of state, outside the jurisdiction of the Church and its bishops.

The Inquisition was set up in 1483 on the authority of a papal bull issued in 1478 (and subsequently much regretted by Rome), but as a royal court with all appointments made by the crown. Its officials were exempt from normal jurisdiction, and its lay assistants functioned as court informers. All proceedings were secret, torture was used to extract confessions, denunciations were encouraged, and the accused were given no right to confront their accusers, who shared with the tribunal and the crown in the proceeds from properties confiscated from those convicted.

Although the number of those convicted was not as great as is often claimed, the Inquisition inspired terror, as it was meant to, and its elaborate public autos-da-fé also inspired feelings of both fear and perverse pleasure on the part of humble citizens who saw many of the rich and mighty abased. By more than four centuries, the Inquisition antedated the thought police and the show trials with public confessions that became a hallmark of twentieth-century totalitarian government.

In the control of education as well, the era of the Catholic monarchs calls to mind the practices of contemporary dictatorships. Early in their reign came a flowering of intellectual and university life, much of it under Italian influence, but with royal and not apostolic guidance. But shortly, the emphasis on secular studies, including law and administration, and humanistic fields began to clash with strict Castilian virtues of *honra*, zealotry, and arrogant righteousness. For the "pure" (castizo) elements of society, the new Italianate learning recalled the old, dangerously alien Judeo-Muslim thought and, like it, was filled with un-Christian content. This was the first time, but not the last, in Spanish history that cosmopolitanism would be lumped together with and considered equivalent to the heresies of minorities.

For this reason, the Renaissance never left a lasting mark on Spain. The cast of Spanish culture was too firmly set in other forms and suspicion of *umanismo* too deeply rooted. The reaction was led by Cardinal Cisneros, archbishop of Toledo, and Grand Chancellor Castile, who determined to consecrate the united kingdom to basic religious values by founding a new university at Alacla de Henares in 1508. The *Complutense,* as described by Alberto Jimenez:

had an essentially ecclesiastical character and came to fill a very important function in the mind of the reformer: to raise the spiritual and cultural level of the regular and secular Spanish clergy by means of a complete organism of primary and higher education. For this reason it was a new institution in every sense, whose destiny could not be tied to the old Universities. (*Historia de la Universidad Española*)

Cardinal Cisneros was associated with other crucial events in this reign: he was instrumental in expelling the Jews in 1492, oversaw the burning of Muslim religious books in Granada (from which he carefully excepted scientific works), convinced the wavering monarchs that Muslims should be forcibly converted, and became general inquisitor in the Holy Office in 1507. He also persuaded the rulers, who were originally to be buried in San Juan de Dios in Toledo, to transfer their mausoleum to Granada as a symbol of their victorius completion of the Reconquest. The inscription on their tomb in the cathedral reflects the true temper of their times:

Ferdinand of Aragon and Isabella of Castile, always husband and wife, called Catholic, lie in this marble tomb. They destroyed the power of the Muhammadan sect and eliminated the obstinacy of the [Jewish] heresy.

The patterns of control (belief and ancestry, education, and the forced expatriation of nonconformists) were perfected in the second half of the sixteenth century by Philip II (1556–98), but not before Spain went through a period in which new ideas coming from abroad briefly did battle with and almost overcame the existing rigid orthodoxy. The reign of Charles I (1516–56), the Hapsburg heir imported from Flanders and deeply distrusted by the local elites, coincided with the beginnings of the Reformation. The new ruler was surrounded by Flemish and Burgundian advisers, and some of his closest retainers became Protestants. Charles himself was accused by Pope Paul IV of having sacrificed orthodoxy to his dream of European hegemony, which included a plan for European religious reconciliation that would enhance his political power.

After the Council of Trent this royal fantasy finally fell apart, and the counterattack of the orthodox was stepped up. It was led at first by the Dominicans, especially Melchor Cano, a delegate at Trent, who castigated all heresies as destructive perversions of the faith and insisted on a clear distinction between formal religion and all deviations from it. His strictures applied primarily to Erasmian humanism, which had many followers in sixteenth-century Spain, and to mysticism, always an important part of the Spanish psyche, which had reappeared among the illuminists (*alumbrados*), many of whom were converted Christians seeking meaningful personal religious experiences and an escape from the stifling nature of orthodoxy.

The two main arms of the revived orthodoxy implanted under Philip II were a broadened Inquisition, essentially a defensive weapon, and the newly founded Society of Jesus, which evolved into a formidable arm of the counterattack. The Inquisition soon destroyed the *alumbrados* and the Erasmians or forced them into exile, and by order of the archbiship of Toledo in 1547 all ecclesiastical appointments were conditioned on blood purity as well as freedom from any accusations of deviance by the Holy Office.

The Jesuits were meant for teaching and missionary work, and to that end they were organized on a hierarchical military pattern: they were to wage war on infidels just as the Inquisition waged it against heretics. The order had close ties to Rome but a distinctly Spanish cast, giving it a bicephalous nature that led to clashes with Philip II on several occasions. Thus it did not reach the apogee of its influence until the early seventeenth century, when it received large sums to found colleges, and especially after 1625 when all teaching in the School of Royal Studies of the Imperial College in Madrid was entrusted to it. The instruction of the children of the highest nobility was henceforth in Jesuit hands for more than a century, and its influence waxed while that of established universities waned and the number of students enrolled in them dwindled to almost none.

Philip II himself, a compulsive clerk in the king's clothes, was virtually a third arm of this neo-orthodoxy. He celebrated his ascent to the throne with the largest auto-da-fé of the century in Valladolid, and in 1559 issued his Pragmatica, forbidding Spaniards to study abroad (and for almost three hundred years no Spanish scholar or scholarly mission did so under official auspices; Spanish soldiers died in Flanders, Milan, and Burgundy, and Spanish diplomats intrigued throughout Europe, but studying and learning abroad were officially prohibited). In the same year he had published the first Spanish index of prohibited books, independent of the Vatican index, thus completing the process of sealing Spain off from European currents of thought.

Spain was thus a part of Europe politically but not intellectually, and this had the most disastrous effect. While European scientific thought developed rapidly in the seventeenth century, by 1650 the University of Salamanca had not one student enrolled in mathematics and by the end of the century not one in medicine.

It is true that art and literature flourished as never before in the brief golden age that lasted until about 1625, but art was either religiously orthodox or royal as in the case of Velazquez a bit later. Literature was subject to scrutiny for subversive tendencies. *Don Quixote* was subversive in the deepest sense, so much so that censors could not see it, and Greco was denounced to the Inquisition for the sensuality of his painting.

In sum, as Spain abandoned the pursuit of objective truth and closed itself in with an ideological dogmatism that paralyzed intellectual life, the long chain of causality that had begun six to seven centuries before came to an end in the late seventeenth century in total sterility. It might equally be called totalitarian sterility, for if totalitarianism is defined as a system that uses state power to impose an official ideology on its subjects, treats nonconformity of thought as resistance to the state, maintains a repressive apparatus of secret police and informers to enforce its proclaimed doctrines, and arrests and tries its presumed opponents in secret and by procedures not subject to any accountability, then Spain from at least the accession of Philip II in 1556 until the coming of the Bourbons in 1700 was a totalitarian state, within the limits imposed at that time by traditional means of control.

Spanish history from the arrival of the Bourbons in 1700 to the Napoleonic invasion of 1808 is subject to different interpretations. It is undeniable that the period was a major turning point, but some Spanish historians consider it a prelude to modern Spanish history whereas others look on it as a kind of entr'acte. Some stress the continuity of bureaucratic practices first put into effect then, and others feel that it was a pause, with a partial opening to the world that failed in the end.

It could also be said that it represented a transition from the theologically centered totalitarianism of the preceding epoch to a rigidly centralized authoritarianism with a more worldly orientation. The changeover extended the range of problems in Spanish society by creating new secular tensions—royal prerogatives, regional differences, and cultural clashes—that existed alongside the old religious exclusivism, which had by no means disappeared. The Jesuits played a leading role in parrying royal power until their expulsion in 1767, and the Inquisition still flourished, although in less virulent form, with almost nine thousand staff members.

Bourbon rule has been described as an adaptation of what was French to a Spanish setting, an importation that ran counter to the Spanish character. But before it recoiled in horror at the events of the French Revolution (notably the execution of other Bourbons) and returned to conservative orthodoxy, it allowed the breath of the Enlightenment to penetrate Spain briefly, principally in the reign of Charles III (1759–88). Royal patronage created museums and academies, reform-minded ministers were appointed, some enlightened nobles brought in foreign instructors in the sciences, and the first voluntary groups devoted to secular intellectual pursuits appeared.

This short-lived burst of progress brought in other imports as well, however: a proliferation of secret societies, a wave of anticlericalism, exotic variants of freemasonry, and an air of libertinism adopted by many *afrancesados* that offended the still deeply conservative bulk of Spanish society, who gradually moved to reject the foreign agents from the body social.

The reaction against alien ways took the form of *casticismo*, a cultural purity standing for what is essentially Spanish and unsullied by foreignisms. It transfers the earlier concepts of religious and ethnic purity to another plane: "Old Christians" are replaced by the "Old Spanish Tradition." Thus *casticismo*, expressing what the Spanish think of as being exclusively and wholly Spanish (when it often is not, as with flamenco), combined with *catolicismo* to provide a structure of cultural-cum-religious unity that was basically isolationist, antiforeign, and antiintellectual, and being essentially Castilian (with appendages from conquered Andalucia)—disdainful of the contributions of the peripheral peoples or Spain: Catalans and Basques, Galicians and Valencians.

The two forces together represented a pastiche of pride, passion, and faith, in which emotion took precedence over reason. The historical importance of the marriage lies in the fact that *castizo-católico* culture for the next two centuries became closely identified with conservative and often immobilist ideas in all aspects of life, while it was opposed by a minority of intellectuals nourished by ideas from abroad and therefore all the more suspect in *castizo* eyes.

Charles III died in 1788, the year before the French Revolution, with many of his reforms stillborn. The Revolution's excesses led all the traditional forces in Spain to strike out against what they thought was the necessary end product of so-called liberal ideas. A blurred blending of what was liberal, foreign, revolutionary, atheist, and heretical gained hold of their minds. A vain rearguard action was fought by the residual followers of the Enlightenment in the 1790s, but the principal response to subversive French ideas was a return to greater intellectual repression and increased censorship. In 1800, a royal decree gave full reign to the Inquisition, which had been required by Charles III to abolish torture and burning at the stake, to prosecute its enemies once again to the fullest.

A lasting result of Bourbon rule and its efforts at reform was a profound division of the country by 1800 into what was thereafter called the "two Spains," one official and the other real. Official Spain began with a conservative majority made up of the court, the clergy, the nobility, and the inertial masses (who, it should be remembered, favored keeping the Jesuits and enjoyed the Inquisition). The real Spain was a liberal minority trying to break the hold that traditional authoritarianism had fastened on the country. The principal theme of nineteenth- and twentieth-century Spain would be the unending antagonism of the two sides, with the conservative majority dwindling and the liberal minority growing as education, industrialization, and urbanization spread with each passing decade.

The subsequent course of Spanish history was overwhelmingly influenced and distorted by the Napoleonic invasion and the Peninsular War that followed (1808–14). Not only was the term *guerrilla* coined then to describe popular resistance, but Spanish mass culture even today ubiquitously uses the theme as its equivalent of the "western," with the guerrillas cast as heroes and the French as villains.

The French shattered ossified institutions at all levels, abolished the Inquisition, reformed the legal system, and brought in the liberal ideas of the French Revolution. But the dilemma was that the change, however beneficial, had been imposed by external force. This caused a national reaction that was literally reactionary: the paradox of a popular rising in favor of a retrograde regime. The unpalatable options for Spaniards were to collaborate with the occupiers in the name of liberalism, to fight them under the banner of obscurantism-cum-nationalism, or to avoid reality, as the framers of the 1812 constitution did in Cádiz, by proclaiming ideals they could not enforce.

The French were finally driven out with British help, and when

Ferdinand VII reclaimed the throne, he reestablished the Inquisition (which held its last execution in 1826 and was finally abolished in 1833), closed the universities, and set up bull-fighting schools throughout the country. The most significant development of those decades was the consolidation of centralized power—just as in Russia and the Ottoman Empire—in a latter-day refeudalization involving an alliance between the crown, large landholders, and a new bourgeoisie investing in land rather than industry, which was left largely in foreign hands.

Brief liberal eras alternated with longer conservative periods through most of the century, with the military intervening through *pronunciamientos* nominally favoring one or the other side but really establishing the tradition that generals were the ultimate arbiters of political matters. Liberal intellectual movements arose, from the *Krausismo* of the 1840s and 1850s, another foreign import, to the *Institución Libre* of Giner de los Rios, but they were under constant attack by conservatives and were held at bay until the last quarter of the century. As late in the day as 1875, liberal university professors were arrested and sent into internal exile by an intransigent minister of education, something unimaginable in any other Western European country at that time.

The weight of greater centralized control and more effective repression, together with the growing strains of nineteenth-century society as rudimentary industrialization got under way, led to two main streams of violent, messianic reaction, both of which played important roles in the unfolding of the Spanish tragedy: one was Carlism, the other anarchism.

Carlism can be understood at different levels of complexity. Superficially, it was a dynastic quarrel about successorial rights; more broadly, an ideological dispute between extreme absolutists and more moderate conservatives; and in the deepest sense, an emotional movement combining both of those features with a spirit of independent regionalism among a rural nobility and a peasantry equally jealous of their traditional rights and suspicious of growing state centralism. In short, it was an intractably Catholic, conservative, regional, and populist movement that took hold among small landholders in the most religious provinces, looking back for a utopia of vanished rural tranquility and the preservation of the socioeconomic status quo.

The rural anarchism of southern Spain's landless peasants was in many ways its mirror image. Shaped by traditions of communal labor on the latifundia and guided by often austere, abstemious leaders inured to hardships, it was akin to a secular religion in which salvation was to be found by achieving communitarian utopian goals. Both rural Carlism and rural anarchism called for the decentralization, if not the disappearance, of the state; the former seeing it as a danger to the individual's time-honored rights, the latter viewing it as a threat to freely constituted communes of farmers and workers. Where they differed crucially, however, was across the significant fault line that (as W. Montgomery Watt showed in pinpointing the essential difference between Shi'ite and Sunni Islam) has marked the thrust of great religious movements at all times: the Carlists believed in salvation through adhering to charismatically virtuous leaders, the anarchists through a charismatically virtuous community.

By 1900, the social reality of Spain was reflected in a more complex fragmentation of forces. Sharp economic and social class divisions were stamped on a still overwhelmingly agrarian society, topped by a small mandarin class at court and among the higher nobility, and only slightly leavened by intellectuals who were unable or unwilling to reach out to the masses. The growth of a sizable middle class, mainly in Catalonia and somewhat less in Madrid, was countered by the appearance of an urban proletariat in and around Barcelona. The tensions of this new quadripartite division of society persisted, and indeed grew, through the decades leading to the final breakdown of the 1930s.

Close to the heart of the problem was the dispute about the place of the church in national life, and the stage on which it would be argued out was increasingly the control of education. The bulk of the aristocratic-bourgeois elite was—as long as their economic privileges were ensured—royalist and nominally Catholic without being too closely bound to the church. This attitude dominated from the restoration of the monarchy in 1874 until around the turn of the century, when it changed as violent, anticlerical radicalism captured the working class of Catalonia, a movement that was a synthesis of the rural anarchism described above and a syndicalism responding to the intolerable social and economic conditions of workers' lives in this newly industrializing region.

The basically apolitical nature of the anarcho-syndicalism made it easier for the many nonreligious workers to direct their hostility toward the church, which was seen as the keystone of the oppressive system, and thus anarcho-syndicalism developed into a broad antiinstitutional, anticlerical, messianic movement capable of mobilizing the strongest emotions and converting them into the most violent acts, as was observed by the now-alarmed establishment during the strikes, riots, and church burnings of the "tragic week" (*semana trágica*) of 1909 in Barcelona, and later with the widespread random terrorism that occurred there for several years after 1917.

Secular revolutionary movements existed elsewhere in Europe at that time, but what marked Spain was not only the fervent anticlericalism expressed but also the forceful reaction to it offered by renewed forces within the church, often referred to as the "neos" (*neo-católicos*), representing an ecclesiastical generation of 1898 wholly distinct from the liberal intellectual movement of the same name.

Although the resurgence of the church in the first decade of this century was galvanized by spreading anticlerical disorders, it had roots going well back into the nineteenth century. The strengthened centralized state at that time had expropriated much of its property, deprived it of much of its income, and limited the number of orders allowed to it. This purge was finally beneficial, however, for whereas the church in the early 1800s had been an overstaffed, parasitical institution living in idleness off its rents, by 1900 it had been trimmed down to a leaner organization concentrating on teaching. After 1887, generally favorable government attitudes permitted new teaching orders to set themselves up, and a major evangelistic effort to recapture the masses got under way, particularly in the Catalan, Asturian, and Valencian regions where the nonreligious proletariat abounded.

This clerical offensive of reproselytization and education went on right up to the fall of the monarchy in 1931. Secular intellectuals were not idle, though. The pioneer work of the *Junta de Ampliación de Estudios* in sending fellows to study abroad, the restructuring of the universities and their dynamic activity up to the military dictatorship of Primo de Rivera in 1923, and the expanded role of a free press, all testify to the vivacity of liberal-secular thought at the time. In addition, instruction aimed specifically at the working class came into vogue: the *Escuela Nueva* of the Socialists and the anarchist schools that flourished in Barcelona until 1909, when the movement was set back for a long time by the violent events of the *semana trágica*.

Thus, three main philosophical streams existed side by side without interacting, reflecting a system that was pluralistic on the surface but was in fact strictly compartmentalized. The church, as Vicens Vives noted, would not abandon "the path it had laid out for itself: the reconquest of society by means of education." The liberals were determined that their vision of secular humanism should be extended to all Spaniards, while the proletariat was increasingly adopting chiliastic and iconoclastic attitudes distinct from and threatening to both. At the top, the moral authority of the state was steadily eroding, as King Alfonso XIII meddled injudiciously in politics. The monarch needed continual support in the form of "fixes," one of which it got in the much-heralded "Union of Throne and Altar," and another in being temporarily shored up by Primo de Rivera (1923–30) before the final collapse.

The Second Republic that followed Alfonso's monarchy was

more than a reform but less than a revolution, and thus it was despised and feared by its enemies on the Right and was dismissed by many of its hypothetical supporters on the Left, who looked on it only as a transition to their own eventual coming to power. It hoped to change everything but finally achieved almost nothing, raising expectations and realizing few of them.

Its program was aimed at moderates, progressives, intellectuals, the professional and middle classes, and skilled workers, precisely the least powerful groups in society. It was undermined from within by the Socialist UGT labor union, inspired by revolutionary Marxism, and on its Left by the anarchist CNT union, driven by the mystique of the ultimate revolution, while it was constantly harassed by traditionalists and Catholics who saw their world being swept away. Finally, it hobbled itself in a typically Spanish way by passionately holding to high principle and refusing to make practical political compromises.

The republic was the beginning of a new era, but one in which the rules that had barely held Spanish society together for more than a century were starting to be changed too drastically and too rapidly. Many of these changes, however much needed to modernize Spanish society, were put into effect in a tactless way that made them even more unacceptable to those who had long held power. After five years of mounting instability and gradually more uncontrollable violence—countless strikes, constant clashes between paramilitary forces of the Left and Right, plots and imagined plots, a bloody insurrection by the extreme Left in Asturias in 1934 put down by the military with an even bloodier retaliation—those traditionalist forces moved in July 1936 to put an end to the social change they detested and to impose a drastic counterchange.

The Spanish experience was unique in Western European history, and important lessons can be learned from it. Although religious intolerance and absolutist rule were commonplace in Europe in many periods, in Spain their causes, duration, and intensity set the country apart. Spain spent long eras in fief to a bigotry that led to control as total as traditional methods could make it, and one sustained far beyond the time when there was any excuse for it. A first conclusion is that prolonged repression ultimately leads to violent reaction—the more extreme the former the more excessive the latter—as happened in Spain from the early nineteenth century onward; and that this reaction leads to counterreaction and a spiral of violence that typically ends, as it did in 1936, in catastrophe.

A corollary of that conclusion is that attempts to establish a visionary society—either a kingdom wholly of God on earth or its converse, a brotherhood of man without God—inflicts unjustifiable suffering and is doomed to disaster. Dogmatic and messianic solutions failed repeatedly in Spanish history, but only recently has this simple truth been realized. The Carlists, now a miniscule group that has moved leftward, are reduced to holding annual picnics at their shrines in the hills of Navarre. The anarchists, with almost no influence in the contemporary labor movement, called a 1983 bank strike, largely unobserved, to protest that time off was not being given on the day of the patron saint of that sector, San Carlo Borromeo. The Falangist remnants are an old boys' club recalling their mostly imaginary glories on the Russian front in World War II. And the Communists, discredited by their infamous treatment of their republican allies in the civil war, are politically marginal, having been held to 5–10 percent of the vote in all elections since 1977, a figure much lower than that in any other southern European country. The injunction to render unto God and Caesar the part devolving on each went unheeded too long, and Spain thus makes an excellent case for the separation of church and state, a concept put into effect for the first time in the Spanish constitution of 1978.

Finally, it might be asked whether a country like Spain is perhaps not better immunized against future despotisms by having gone through its painful historical experience. If so, Spain must be content to "pay and indefinitely to go on paying" the price of the goods it has finally chosen. And that payment includes remembrance as well as vigilance.

That payment also means working umremittingly to build a more equitable community. From being a society in which laws were meant to be ignored by some and bent by others, and people to be bribed or nepotized, it must proceed to more impersonal standards of rectitude. From extremes of fanaticism and destructiveness it must learn to divide between Caesar and God—with not too much for either and a goodly part saved for imperfect human beings. And from being a society of segmented entities, in which people had bitterly learned to be wary of the state, its agents, and all "others," it must develop a sense of thoughtful participation and measured integration, and of mutual trust. All this it is painfully beginning to do, so much so that if Orwell did come back to Spain in 1984 he would be amazed by what he saw, but I think that beyond any question he would like it.

BEYOND TRIBAL ALLEGIANCE: THE INDIAN CITIZEN

LADONNA HARRIS

The relationship between the United States and American Indians has long been characterized by conflict, controversy, and legal complexity. In the early years, the conflict erupted into military confrontation. More recently, the battle is waged in courts of law. It is a conflict that should concern all Americans because it reflects society's acceptance of plurality principles within its system of government. More than a philosophical issue is involved here, however. Over the past two hundred years, an entire body of law has developed dealing exclusively with the rights of the Indian in the United States. Moreover, the way the United States behaves toward the American Indian has far-reaching implications as to how it will behave toward other ethnic groups both at home and in other nations of the world.

What is the conflict? Simply put, the question is one of governance. The Indian asserts, desires, and demands the right to exist as an Indian, the right to organize distinctively Indian systems of government within the context of traditional tribal and cultural values.

On the other hand, the United States is in the business of governing Americans—people who are American first and who only secondarily—if at all—identify ethnically. Over the years, many strategies have been employed to instill this sense of Americanness in the Indian. Most of those strategies have had the reverse effect, however, and the result has been to make Indian people hold dearer their right to internal tribal sovereignty and self-determination.

The right of tribal governments to exist as politically distinct units of government is real. In the legal sense, it stems from the doctrine of aboriginal rights, which provides a somewhat ill-defined guideline to protect aboriginal inhabitants during a period of colonization. On a more practical level, insofar as American Indian tribal governmental rights are concerned, it grew from a real need for military and economic allies by a fledgling United States.

During the colonial period of U.S. history, little was known about the interior of the continent, making it difficult for the colonial government to exploit effectively the vast resources available. Furthermore, the tribes did not take kindly to outsiders encroaching upon their established territories. Another problem centered around the fact that competing European interests had also carved out pieces of the continent for their own exploitation and were not hesitant to seek out Indian military assistance. The Indians had an effective military that they too were not ill disposed to utilize if the need arose.

As a result, it served the interests of the young nation to find a mechanism through which to establish friendly relations with the Indian nations. A treaty was a familiar mechanism and became the primary vehicle for U.S.-Indian alliances and agreements until the late nineteenth century. However, in order to execute a valid treaty, the agreeing parties must both represent sovereign nations. To do so, the United States recognized the validity of the Indians' status as nations with all the rights and responsibilities that statehood entails. The U.S. Constitution enshrined this concept by language referring to Indian nations. It is doubtful that such language would have been included had it not been the intent of the framers to deal with the tribes on a government-to-government basis.

As times change, however, so do attitudes and interest. U.S.-Indian relations began to deteriorate in direct proportion to the increase of the population. By the 1830s, the deterioration reached a crisis point. The United States was anxious to settle the southeastern quarter of the continent, but the Cherokee, Choctaw, Seminole, Chickasaw, and Creek nations occupied this region and defended their right to the land in a federal court. In 1831, Chief Justice John Marshall in *Cherokee Nation v. Georgia* delivered a landmark decision holding that the Indian tribes are sovereign domestic dependent nations under federal law. This was founded upon the treaty relationship established earlier and meant that tribes retained all the sovereign governmental authorities of an independent nation, except those powers specifically prohibited by Congress or voluntarily resigned to the United States by treaty. Incidentally, this decision continues to be the basis for tribal claims of governmental authority today.

In spite of this tremendous victory in the Supreme Court, the southeastern tribes—more colorfully known as the "Five Civilized Tribes" because of their acceptance of "civilized ways"—were given the choice of moving west of the Mississippi River or losing their sovereign status. Unfortunately, President Andrew Jackson and the Congress did not concur with the Supreme Court's ruling, finding it inconsistent with notions of state sovereignty and national policy. In 1834, the Congress unburdened the tribes of this decision by passing the Indian Removal Act, which authorized the forcible removal of Indians to Indian territory, now the state of Oklahoma.

The removal policy was to be short lived, however, because as the United States continued to expand westward it became impossible to continue to resettle Indians to the west of white settlements. Unlike their cousins to the east, the western tribes were not anxious to adopt "civilized ways" for, at the time, they were enjoying an era of unprecedented tribal cultural growth and prosperity. The horse had liberated the Indian, and tribal life flourished. Western tribes were also well aware of the unhappy fate that befell the eastern tribes as a result of their trust in white settlers' ways.

Both sides understood that some type of agreement was needed to serve the interests of all, if armed conflict was to be avoided. The United States proposed to honor the sovereignty of tribes within a clearly defined boundary of land on a reservation. A treaty was to be negotiated that would contain the terms of the arrangement between each affected tribe and the United States. Thus began the reservation era.

Although the establishment of reservations seriously reduced the size of tribal territories, the original reservation boundaries were quite large. Sacred lands were retained, and the Indians were sufficiently satisfied to contain their activities to areas within the established borders. Moreover, it was generally felt among Indians that their military strength was sufficient to repel further encroachment.

Events leading up to the Civil War slowed westward expansion for a few years but also dramatically increased the size and sophistication of the U.S. military in a way that was to become fatal for the Indian. As soon as the war ended, the westward rush was on. Overwhelming numbers of white settlers began pouring into the interior of the continent, into Indian country.

The billowing white canvases of the Conestoga wagon were not an entirely new sight to the Indian. Gold was discovered in 1849, and streams of white people passed through Indian territory on their way to riches. After the Civil War, the whites were no longer just passing through; they were staying in ever increasing numbers. Soon they began to encroach upon tribal lands. Convinced of the worst, tribes across the continent resorted to military force to protect their boundaries, finally suffering defeat at the hands of the U.S. Cavalry and ultimately losing a drastic amount of tribal territory through treaties, statutes, and executive orders.

The years immediately following the cessation of military hostilities were especially miserable for the American Indian. The Indian economy had been destroyed. Great buffalo herds, which had formed the basis of the Indian economy for most tribes inhabiting the great central plains, were gone. Other game had been seriously depleted, and most tribes were confined to reservations that were much smaller than promised and considered undesirable for non-Indian settlement. The Indian people became almost totally dependent on federal aid for subsistence.

It was the expense of this dependency that prompted the federal government to reassess Indian policy. Congress took careful note of the "Indian problem." Isolation was not working, and Indians still held some fairly sizable chunks of prime farmland. Assimilation became the buzzword of the time.

It was a time to Americanize the Indian. In 1887, Congress passed the General Allotment (Dawes) Act, which divided reservations into 160-acre tracts to be allotted to every living adult member of the tribe. Once the allotment process was complete, the so-called surplus lands were to be sold to non-Indian settlers. The allotments were to become inalienable and nontaxable for a period of twenty-five years, in order to allow the allottee to become accustomed to this new way of life. Interestingly, the act conferred citizenship upon each allottee, but this was later overturned by the Supreme Court.

Actually, however, it amounted to one of the largest land grabs in history, and the effect it had on tribal governing authority was devastating. It substantially reduced the amount of land over which tribes exercised sovereign authority and led to a breakdown of traditional tribal governing systems. In 1887, Indian landholdings amounted to some 140 million acres. Within forty years, approximately 90 million of those acres had passed into non-Indian ownership.

Over the course of the next thirty years, many more assimilationist tribal statutes were enacted, including the Major Crimes Act, which gave jurisdiction over the ten most common crimes to the federal courts. In 1871, the treaty-making process was terminated. In 1924, all Indians were granted U.S. citizenship.

Prior to 1924, approximately sixty thousand Indians had been granted citizenship status. This followed the 1906 Supreme Court decision that ruled those allotted lands under the 1887 General Allotment Act could only become citizens after the twenty-five-year trust period over the lands had expired. Several other citizenship statutes had been passed during this same period. All were conditioned on proof that the Indians were of "sufficient prudence and intelligence to conduct their affairs and interests" or "abandon their tribal relations, adopt the habits of civilized life, become self-supporting and learn to read and write English." Also, Indian veterans of World War I and Indian women upon marriage to non-Indian men were granted citizenship.

The Indian Citizenship Act finally put an end to special requirements and criteria and provided the basis for a Supreme Court ruling that tribal participation and membership was compatible with U.S. citizenship. Some may find it surprising that the citizenship legislation was not a major interest on the part of the Indian tribes. In fact, many Indians argued that citizenship should not be imposed without individual consent, but the argument was rejected by the Supreme Court.

Slowly, the trend shifted again with a 1928 report that contributed to more equitable policies regarding the rights of tribal peoples and tribal governments. Familiarly known as the Merriam report, it documented the abysmal conditions that existed on reservations stemming from the paternalistic administration of Indian affairs by the Interior Department. The report recommended encouraging Indian use of their own lands and strengthening Indian community life and culture. The Merriam report initiated a policy shift that led ultimately to legislation that ended the allotment process and stressed the consolidation of tribal lands, the preservation of tribal heritage, and the revitalization of tribal governments.

The passage of the Indian Reorganization Act of 1934 (IRA) is generally viewed as a positive development. However, some have criticized the IRA for being responsible for the disillusionment with distinctively Indian forms of government and substituting "white man's law for old tribal ways," because the IRA established nontraditional tribal councils with broad authorities. Most of the criticism, however, was directed at the extensive control retained by the federal government over IRA governments through the veto power of the Interior secretary over council enactments. This veto power is not found in the IRA, but in the tribal constitutions drafted by the Bureau of Indian Affairs.

In the 1950s, the policy of strengthening tribal governments was interrupted by an era of termination legislation, which typically ended the special relationship between the federal government and the tribes and discontinued federal programs for Indians. The legislation imposed state authority over the former reservation lands and subjected the land to state taxes. The land was often sold with proceeds distributed among tribal members or placed in a private trust. Though nothing in the termination acts expressly ended tribal sovereignty, the effect was the same since tribes no longer had a land base over which to assert jurisdiction. In many ways, the termination policies were a return to nineteenth-century attitudes that Indians should be freed from federal supervision and control and from limitations specifically applicable to Indians. The period lasted from 1954 to 1962 and affected nearly one hundred tribes. In every instance, terminated tribes suffered drastic economic and social problems directly linked to the withdrawal of federal concern and support for Indian rights.

Recognizing that the termination policies were utterly debilitating, President Lyndon Johnson sent a special message to Congress in 1968 stressing that "self-determination for tribes is the goal that erases old attitudes of paternalism and promotes partnership and self-help." President Richard Nixon went the next step and formally sought congressional repudiation of the termination policy; he proposed legislation passing responsibility for certain federal programs to tribes, and he proposed Indian control of Indian schools. The president's recommendations were enacted into law in the Indian Self-Determination and Education Act of 1975. Self-determination continues to be the overriding policy of the United States toward Indians and was most recently reaffirmed by President Ronald Reagan.

Shifts in policies, political and social attitudes, and legal thought have a profound influence on Indian life, ensuring an active and vocal assertion of the rights of citizenship. Unlike any other ethnic group in the United States, Indians possess a dual citizenship—entitled to the federal services provided to all citizens as well as to special services because of their status as Indians. Indian tribal governments are a real part of the the American political fabric because of their status as governments.

Beyond strict definition of law, Indian tribal governments provide some interesting interpretations of the responsibility of citizens and of governments. On the tribal level, one cannot be divorced from the responsibilities for one's actions. Cultural and familiar linkages are extremely close. The Indian culture demands certain standards of behavior.

To live as a people remains a legacy of times long past. Cultural attitudes persist, and the Indian works diligently to balance the old with the new in all areas of life: social, political, economic, spiritual, or artistic. Indian people are well aware of the challenges that confront them in this age of computers, rockets, advanced telecommunications, and space shuttles, yet deep inside, Indians believe it is possible to reconcile the new with the old.

3

CONSTITUTIONALISM IN DAILY LIFE

BEYOND TRIBAL ALLEGIANCES: PLAYING TO WIN

JOSÉ ANTONIO JÁUREGUI

Some animals are more equal than others.

George Orwell, *Animal Farm*

In 1977, Manuel Martin, a well-known Spanish journalist, interviewed me on a television program called "Hour Fifteen" about my book, *The Rules of the Game: The Tribes.* "Professor Jáuregui," he said, "I'm rather baffled by your general claim that man—any man, every man—is genetically and culturally programmed to play games in order to win and to create dynamic hierarchies. But, dear professor, everybody except you would agree that we are entering more and more into an era of equality, or at least of greater equality. Was not the French Revolution a step toward *l'égalité?* Didn't slavery disappear? Didn't feudalism vanish from the scene? Haven't dictatorships given way to democracy? Is not mankind progressing from the dark ages of domination into an era of equality? What is more: is not there an interest, a desire, an ethic impulse toward equality? My dear professor: you seem to ignore history. You don't seem to realize that mankind is not an unchanging structure, an inevitably rigid beehive. Is it?"

"Well," I replied, "even those who claim they are struggling for equality are in fact trying to win another game, created precisely on the excuse of a pretended equality: they are trying to prove that they are ethically superior to those who aren't fighting for equality.

"It seems to me that both sperms and politicians are programmed to play the same game: the game of winning and losing—the egg in one instance, the White House in the other. All Americans—all men—are created equal in front of God. So are the sperms. Before the game, all men or sperms are equal. So far, equality rules. But once the sperms start running in the vagina or Americans start down the presidential road, all are pushed by strong mechanisms to win. The winner of the egg or of the White House will no longer be equal. He will be number one. The purpose of any game is precisely to destroy former equality and to create dynamic hierarchy."

After I returned home a senator phoned me from Barcelona: "Jáuregui, I know that politicians are a debased species, but you went a bit far. You have degraded us to the level of sperms." I replied, "I just got an irate complaint from the IUS, International Union of Sperms. The sperms feel they have been defamed, insulted, for having been compared to politicians. At least—as a sperm put it to me—we are honest. We admit we run to win. Politicians, on the contrary, rarely admit they run to win, to defeat another. They claim they look for greater equality and all kinds of false pretenses. They run for an egg like us, but they won't admit it."

Is the sperm right? Is George Orwell right when he claims that one form of hierarchy is only replaced by another, but hierarchy itself is never replaced? Can nature be altered by the human will? Is nature the last puppeteer, manipulating sperms and humans to live as players trying to defeat each other in games that create hierarchy or domination? Is only culture—certain cultures at any rate—responsible for human games leading to dynamic hierar-

chies? Is just the wicked human individual—Nero, Hitler, Stalin—
or a group of individuals, such as the aristocratic or bourgeois
class, responsible for inequality, domination, and exploitation?

I have tried so far to answer these fascinating and baffling questions that fascinated and baffled George Orwell, in two of my published books: *The Rules of the Game: The Tribes* and *The Rules of the
Game: The Sexes.* The names of both books are not simply "catchy."
The *game* is one of the main issues. The *rules* of the game is the
other. The *anthropos,* the human being, is programmed both genetically and culturally. Each is a player in order to escape equality, in
order to prove superior to "the others."

Psychic mechanisms, like the urge to win, push the *anthropos* of
all times and of all cultures to play all kinds of games. The urge to
eat, to defecate, or to win is a biosocial mechanism, a psychic
mechanism that works with full autonomy from individual conscience and will. I have called these psychic mechanisms *unconscious* (i.e., working with full autonomy from our conscience) and
abulic (i.e., working with full autonomy from our will). The urge to
win, like the urge to eat—like any psychic mechanism—works at
three times: before the action (or game), during the action, and
after the action. Before eating, the urge to eat pushes the *anthropos*
with invisible but very real hands toward doing a precise operation. It is both a promise of receiving a psychic reward ("If you eat
now, you'll get this kind and amount of pleasure") and an uncom-
fortable feeling that will increase as long as the operation is de-
layed. Likewise, before the game, the human is pushed to play and
to win with both impulses: a promise of reward and a nagging
feeling while not entering the game.

During the action, eating or playing is already being rewarded
("the game is exciting"). Finally, after eating or winning, a final
reward is paid: satisfaction derived from accomplishment. The difference in the process of eating and of playing is that playing is by
nature social and cruel, while eating is individual and unharmful to
others. One can enjoy eating without having to make others suffer,

but nobody can win the game without making the losers suffer. The psychic reward that Reagan got while winning is proportional to the psychic suffering automatically inflicted to Carter. This is one of the inevitable biosocial laws of any game. The winner of the Nobel Prize, of the presidential election, or of the game of sanctity necessarily achieves a psychic reward proportional to the psychic penalty inflicted upon the losers.

In academic and profane circles we admit or take for granted that there are two kinds of human societies: *savage* or *primitive* societies and *civilized* ones. Still, there are several kinds of human societies; they differ not only in degree but in nature. Karl Marx argues that the history of humankind "until now" (when he writes *The Communist Manifesto* and *Das Capital*) is a history of class struggle. He defines *classes* as *patricians* and *plebeians* (Roman society), *feudal lords* and *serfs* (European Middle Ages), or *bourgeois* and *proletarians*. It is undeniable—I suppose we owe this discovery to Marx—that our species is divided into classes, and that indeed these human societies are "struggling" (my concept of "game"). But, what are we talking about when we affirm that "America defeated Japan," "Britain won the war with Argentina," "Spain won the Nobel Prize this year?" What kind of human societies are Spain, America, Japan, Britain, or Argentina? Are they classes?

It is imperative that we take notice of these two kinds of human societies: the class and the tribe. A *class* is a human society identified with material wealth. The frontier between patricians and plebeians is money. A *tribe*, on the other hand, is a human society identified with a bordered territory. The key of a class is money, while the key of a tribe is land.

Humans play their social games with their classes as well as with their tribes. These games may not necessarily coincide. They can even be opposed. A contemporary English "worker" may be involved in a social game with an Argentinian "worker"—in the Malvinas/Falkland game. Both belong, as "workers," to the same class. According to Marx, "Workers do not have homeland." Yet, I find that whenever a human being gets involved in a struggle between one tribe and another (whether in the field of soccer or war), class is irrelevant. Workers do have a homeland. The English worker sees, thinks, and feels English in front of the Argentinian worker. The game of tribes prevails over the game of classes. War, soccer, and many other games (including international scientific competitions in which the tribal game may be somehow present) melt all classes into a single territorial team.

There is another kind of human society, what I would call the "ideological society," that is often confused with a class. The ideological society is a human society identified with a policy or ethical program. A left-wing duke belongs to the same social team as a poor left-wing worker. Both profess the same faith, the same ideals, the same dogmas; both venerate the same ideological heroes (i.e., both may have in their homes a portrait of Marx; the one that hangs in the left-wing duke's palace is painted by a fashionable painter and is worth thousands of dollars, whereas the left-wing worker's Marx portrait is worth a few dollars). The left-wing duke lives in a palace, drives a Rolls, eats in expensive restaurants, drinks champagne, buys mink coats for his mistress, and will rest in peace in an upper-class grave in an upper-class cemetery. The worker's life is quite different.

When will an English left-wing duke join his tribal fellows, instead of his classmates or his ideological comrades? We should not answer hastily. In the Spanish civil war, the two principal rival teams were split largely on ideological grounds. Marxist upper, middle, and working classes joined the same ideological team and together played the game of war. When Napoleon invaded Spain in 1808, all classes and all ideological teams joined the territorial team—Spain—against the *Franchutes* (a derogatory Spanish reference to the French). Yet in ordinary life, workers, whether left- or right-wing, never meet upper-class people even when they belong to the ideological team.

Are we, then, going toward greater equality or are some still "more equal than others," as Orwell put it? The more humankind has walked in the path of history, the more it has been compelled to play games. Humans are called upon to prove their superiority. Everywhere—including the Soviet Union—we find them trying to win the games of housing, decorating, dressing, sitting in better seats at the theater, in a train, in a boat, or on a plane, even having a more distinguished funeral, a better place to rest in the cemetery. The game never ends. It is said that death makes all men equal, but not quite. People are still interested in the game after death. Even after death, they are pushed to prove their superiority. When Bach is composing, Velázquez painting, or an unknown citizen trying to kill a president, are they not hearing inside themselves the question: "Will you enter posterity?"

People seem to be fashioned by nature with these biosocial, psychic mechanisms that push them to play and to win. Culture adds new dimensions to these games. Writing, painting, and composing are cultural creations that have invented new games and new hierarchies. Writers, painters, and composers are pushed to play these cultural games, to win, and to proclaim their superiority. What is more, whenever someone has tried to create greater equality, a new game and a new hierarchy has been made. Christianity or Marxism seem to be doctrines aimed at creating greater equality: "that all are equal in front of God" (Christianity) or "let us eliminate the classes and exploitation of humans by each other" (Marxism). Yet Christianity creates two new games and two new dynamic hierarchies: one on earth and one after death "in the other world." On this earth a new hierarchy appears: the pope, the cardinals, the bishops, the priests, and the laypeople. In the other world: the saints (those who won the game of their lives), the saved (a middle class who won the game but finished behind the saints), and the eternally condemned who go to Hell (they lost the game on earth). Marxism creates the secretary general (the number one of the beehive), the politburo (the cardinals, or great executives), and then the mathematically graded party members in a precise pecking order of prestige and power.

Of these three human societies—the class, the ideology, the tribe—the tribe is the most powerful and the most sophisticated. It comprises several kinds of territorial societies. When the Romans gave a single name to a particular territory, Hispania, they started the creation of a new territorial society. Those who reside in this territory become *hispani*. However, the *hispani* of the Roman Empire had nothing else in common. To have in common a new name is not a lot, yet it may be a beginning. A new territorial team starts its existence identified as *hispani* as opposed to the *nonhispani* (i.e., members of territorial societies outside the borders of the territory marked with the sound, concept, and feeling of *Hispania*). Other subsequent games continued the fashioning and growth of Hispania. The Moors arrive with a new ideology or religion and with powerful weapons that they use to persuade others about the truth of their faith. The small Christian kingdoms of Castile, Aragon, Navarre, Leon, and others work as territorial teams equipped with important territorial mechanisms of unity: same name, same coat of arms, same king, and same army. Yet a new ideological and military team starts after the invasion of the Moors in the eighth century: the Christian team against the Moorish team. Hispania, after being just a nominal team, starts to become something else: an ideological-religious team, a military team, a linguistic team. The *hispani* have not yet a common political or military leader, but there is a common urge to defeat the invading Moors. Early in this game between Christians and Moors, the new leader appears: Santiago Matamoros, Saint James the Killer of Moors.

Even today Saint James appears in the cathedrals of Spain dressed as a soldier on a horse having cut off the neck of a Moor who lies bleeding at the feet of his horse. The family name Matamoros, "killer of Moors," is fairly common in Spain. Many churches and cities are called Santiago, both in Spain and in America. The king of Spain, every year on Saint James's day—a national holiday—kneels down in the Cathedral of Saint James to thank him publicly in the name of Spain. He is invoked as the patron saint of Spain, who still looks after the unity and prosperity of Spain. This is how a territorial team develops into a cultural imperative.

A territorial society that has become a sophisticated team (economic-political-military, possibly cultural and ideological or religious) also develops a sophisticated *totemic cult*. A *totem* is any object or person that is venerated by the members of a territorial society not because of its intrinsic qualities but because it represents symbolically the territorial society itself. Citizens venerate their nation, represented symbolically by a flag, a mere piece of cloth. They react harshly to those who would mistreat their flag. An Iranian burns an American flag; the brain computer of an American immediately translates these sensations into ideas and feelings: "This alien is insulting my territorial society: America," and a feeling of anger is triggered. So the Stars and Stripes say: "I am America." The current queen of England would also be right if she said, "I am England."

The totem—whether an object or a person—provides an emotional symbol that floods both the territory and the brain archives of the members of this territory. The flag marks the brain archives: each time that the ocular cameras pick it up the brain computer files this image as well as its translation into an idea or feeling. Likewise, images of the king, queen, president, or other leader may flood the territory and brain computers on coins, bank notes, and stamps. Like the flag, a king, queen, or president may be the object of an elaborate cult in sophisticated and rhythmic rituals.

One of the differences between a flag and a human being is that a piece of cloth cannot think: "Good Heavens! I must be somebody for being venerated and adored in this way." But any Hitler, any Mao, or any Stalin may have this thought. Some analysts argue that to have a queen, like the current queen of England, is entirely useless because she has no real political power. We could equally ask: What does a flag do for a country? The point is that no territorial society can work without symbols and rituals.

It is not useless to have a separation, such as in England, of the totem and the leader. The person who plays the role of the totem cannot play the role of the leader (prime minister). The person who plays the leader cannot, on the other hand, play the role of the totem. The English prime minister's image cannot enter the coins, bank notes, stamps, or portraits in schools and embassies, since all these places are already occupied with the image of the queen.

Hitler, Stalin, Mao, and Franco built up their totalitarian power on the basis of the totemic cult. Every Hitler starts flooding the territory with his image. He tries to channel toward himself the love for Germany, the territorial society. It is basically a tribal phenomenon. It is not rigorous enough to attribute the totalitarian power of Hitler to his maniac personality.

Separating totem and leader in the political system may be important. Possibly, in a system like that in the United Kingdom today, it is harder for a Hitler or a Mao to rise as a dictator. Still, it is obvious that a U.S. president plays the role of both a totem and a leader. That is why a U.S. president is far more powerful than a British prime minister. A British prime minister has no right of veto, can be attacked by a vote of censure in Parliament, and cannot derive any power for symbolically representing England. However, other important independent powers may avoid the totalitarian temptations of a U.S. president: an independent press, an independent Congress, and an independent judicial system. But it is undeniable that President Reagan equaled Queen Elizabeth plus Margaret Thatcher. To ignore the totemic cult and totemic power at any rate in a contemporary territorial society is to miss an important mechanism of the political system and to miss one of the crucial keys to explaining the so-called personality cult, as well as the totalitarian powers, of Stalin, Hitler, or Mao.

The species owes much to England, to France, to the Soviet Union, to America, to Japan, to India, to Spain, to the existence and game of territorial, ideological, and other societies. Without England, our species would be less, and less as well without America. Yet *1984*'s message of somber and apocalyptic events is far from an imagined bad dream. Tribes have created much but also have destroyed much. The key words in politics today are words like *democracy, freedom, equality,* and *communism*. Nice words that do not fit the facts of real politics.

Politics is basically a struggle of tribes. The freedom of Americans does not coincide with the freedom of Soviets. The freedom of any territorial society does not coincide with the freedom of others. When we talk about democracy we overlook this crucial fact. Every tribe is forever struggling with all others to become number one. The world pie—bread, power, and prestige—is the object of dispute among tribes at all times. The game has not changed in nature, only in its sophistication.

War is the parent of any territorial society in three ways: (1) a new tribe often owes its existence to a war won; (2) a tribe owes its maintenance to celebration with elaborate rituals of the wars won; and (3) a tribe owes its existence, power, and prosperity to the capability of its military power. A superpower or an empire is a supermilitary power. Immanuel Kant said that "no nation will qualify as civilized while possessing any army." Are we still in a savage, tribal era of humankind, in which the war of tribes is the crucial game, the key of politics? Are we inevitably doomed to a genetic game of tribal confrontation that we cannot escape?

We must admit that any human being is genetically and culturally programmed as *Homo tribalis*—American, Spanish, French, whatever. Complex mechanisms make any human being think and feel as a player or fan of one territorial team. He or she cannot avoid feeling hurt if the territorial team loses a Nobel Prize, a football championship, or a war. To deny this biosocial program seems to ignore the essential rules of the human game.

Yet, this is only one side of the coin. On the flip side, we seem to be in fact unique animals because we worry about ethical questions. We are built with opposed programs: "Forgive your enemies; love your neighbors as yourself." The two programs in fact keep battling in their own intense and fierce game. Are we becoming more universal or more tribal? We are becoming both. Each new invention has made humans more universal and yet more tribal. Printing has become a common possession of humankind. Yet printing has allowed *Homo tribalis* to create passports and visas better to protect our territorial borders. Planes turn humankind into global villagers. The planet is ours. New inventions have turned the skies and the seas into territorial spaces, into territorial waters. Once tribes fought their war games only on land; now, on land, sea, air, and perhaps soon in space. *Homo universalis* wins some battles, but so does *Homo tribalis.* Marshall McLuhan said that media have turned humankind into a global village. This again is only one side of the coin. One hears today in France: "This is the world news at 10:00," but in fact one hears that 90 percent of the news is about France, and only 10 percent is on other tribes. *Le Monde* means "the world", but in fact again this newspaper is feeding the brain of its readers with territorial ideas and feelings about *la France.* Each time there is a new intervention, if *Homo universalis* advances, *Homo tribalis* advances too.

Whenever *Homo universalis* has launched new universal ideologies, *Homo tribalis* has counterattacked. Marxism has become Chinese Marxism against Soviet Marxism. Two ever-opposed territorial societies, the Soviet Union and China, today use Marxism as another territorial game they did not have before. Allah, Jahveh, Christ, and Saint James may become at any time the invisible leader of a territorial team playing a war against another. Religion, as a universal phenomenon, turns into a tribal game.

Animal Farm and *1984* do not invite us, I suppose, to simply cross our arms and accept an inevitable fate of doom and misery. The message of George Orwell would rather be: "We are all in the battle of light and darkness. The rules of the game have not changed. Whatever the time and tribe, humans are always human. The new techniques, however, make people each time more free and yet subject to new dangers of totalitarianism. Let us be ever on the alert. Let us not be deceived by totalitarian forces disguised as ethnic liberations." The main message of Orwell is perhaps to be alert not to swallow beautiful ethical doctrines that in fact disguise forms of human exploitation.

THE FAMILY FARM: A SUCCESS STORY WITH GLOBAL IMPLICATIONS

ORVILLE L. FREEMAN

Among the overarching concepts and deeply challenging concerns about human freedom and technology, the family farm would seem to be a minor theme, both parochial and pragmatic. In fact, however, the family farm, its history, and its meaning for the world illustrate and even illuminate three of the most fundamental issues raised by those concerns.

First, are human freedom and technology natural enemies? The family farm is a practical manifestation—down to earth, in the most complete meaning of that much-abused metaphor—of how high technology and human freedom can be and must be melded for optimum results.

Second, can humans give up short-term gratification in favor of future planning? The family farm is almost a classic case history of what I think of as the Rohatyn Proposition, namely that societies and economies are successful to the degree that they can forego immediate satisfaction if necessary to make provision for the future. Putting this into language that every family farmer recognizes as basic reality, a successful farmer cannot eat the seed corn.

Finally, is technology morally neutral? The family farm experience answers this intriguing question unequivocally, in that technology inspires and infuses a clear set of values in farm society. In all societies, whatever the cultural context, technology is a response to human need. And if you accept the fact, as I do, that meeting human needs is a desirable undertaking, and as such profoundly moral, technology is not neutral. It is a positive force.

Having placed the family farm in these transcendental dimensions, let me now put it into more practical perspective by offering some definitions of what the family farm is and what is it not. Some seductive mythmaking and romantic nostalgia notwithstanding, the family farm is not a pastoral, idyllic arrangement in which people are made better by communing with nature and being close to the soil and the elements. Family farmers can be as parochial and irrational, self-centered and passionately wrong headed, as any other segment of the population. What is true about the family farm is that it constitutes a solid base to measure, test, and evaluate social and political phenomena in a framework that assumes free choice and that recognizes that choice is most free when the object chosen is directed to the benefit of the individual or to the benefit of someone with whom that person has close bonds.

Another popular notion that needs to be dispelled is that a family farm is the same as a small farm. Far too often, farm discussions and farm programs idealize the small farmer and express regret that the traditional American farm, defined as 40 acres and a mule, is no more. This is not to say that farm units of this size no longer exist—even in the United States—or that they or the people who work on them do not warrant concern. But it is important to realize that the family farm has an economic definition that is clear and concise even though, like other successful economic units, it varies in magnitude. A definition of the family farm that is meaningful in both economic and social terms, and that applies anywhere in the world, is a farm that is operated by one family with no more than one and one-half man-years of outside labor and utilizes the agricultural technology necessary to become an effective economic unit that can earn its way in the world's competitive marketplace.

In the United States today, a family farm is a fairly large unit, and the size has grown over the years. The "40 acres and a mule" definition passed into history with the nineteenth century. In 1920, an American family farm constituted roughly 180 acres. In 1980, it was closer to 450 acres. And these are broad-brush averages. Today a family farm, in the economic, operational definition, can vary from 10 acres for a truck or vegetable farm to 2,500 acres for a wheat farm. But it is these economically determined family farms that make up the overwhelming percentage of agricultural productivity in the United States, a productivity that constitutes a miracle of American agriculture unmatched anywhere on the globe or anytime in history.

It is a miracle that can be measured. Only a hundred years ago, U.S. agriculture was subsistence agriculture, with 80 percent of all Americans living on the land. Today, 2.2 million farm families, totaling 6 million persons, feed the American people better and more cheaply than any other people on the planet and feed additional millions of others in the rest of the world as well. Food from America's family farms has reached hungry people under a wide variety of programs including, on a global scale, the Food for Peace program and, domestically, others such as school-lunch programs, food stamps for the needy, and food for shut-ins, pregnant women, and young children. The fact that some of these programs are under attack today for inequities and inefficiencies that have perhaps distorted their original intention does not change the fact that they have made an important contribution—and continue to make such a contribution—to the welfare of humankind.

In another measure of the phenomenal success story of the American family farm, as late as 1940, each American farm family was capable of feeding ten persons. Today, the average American farm family can feed seventy-seven.

One other widely held and thoroughly erroneous notion about the family farm requires correction. It is a fiction that constitutes the other side of the rosily romantic, bucolic fantasy. In that myth, the family farmer is an unsophisticated rube, with limited intellectual horizons, pursuing an essentially simple and simpleminded task. People who view the family farm in this light believe that agriculture is a primitive process in which you dig a hole, throw some seed into the ground, sprinkle a little fertilizer on it, and get results. This is not only untrue; it is a dangerous misconception. The truth of the matter is that agriculture is highly complex and difficult. It is also subject to complicated political, emotional, sociological, and anthropological forces that vary with the traditions of different areas, countries, localities, and tribes. Agricultural management requires the most sophisticated and up-to-date techniques and equipment.

Indeed, today, from a production-process point of view in agriculture, we need to think in terms of systems engineering. The system must include land, reasonably knowledgeable people, credit, and inputs such as seeds, fertilizer, chemicals, water, and a suitable climate. You have to be able to harvest the crop within sharp time frames. You have to be able to store it so that it does not deteriorate. You then have to move it to a processing plant, so it can become food. And then you have to move the product to market. It is a long, complicated, involved, convoluted chain.

In addition, agriculture today is at the forefront of technological advance. Biogenetics and allied technologies have the potential of changing human lives and improving human welfare, not only in the United States but also around the globe, in a manner and at a pace that parallels the role and effect of computers. Richard Critchfield, a sensitive and knowledgeable expert on rural development worldwide, argues, and I concur, that "one can now confidently say that a quiet agricultural revolution has begun that is likely to have more dramatic effects on more human beings than any revolution that has gone before."

Orville L. Freeman   130

Critchfield also notes, and again I can confirm this from personal experience, that "biological technology is a chapter just begun." This is true in the United States, but, equally as important from a planetary perspective, it is also true in the Third World, where the overwhelming majority of the planet's people live. Critchfield points out—and once more I can corroborate this from my own experience—"the best-informed sources on the Third World in the 1980s, I find, are agricultural scientists: the agronomists, plant breeders, soil men and such who have been quietly changing the face of world agriculture the past 15 years." Most of them are connected with the new international network linking thirteen agricultural research centers, eight of them set up since 1971. Scientists in national programs in 130 developing countries are participating. Since the Chinese became actively involved during the late 1970s, this network has been pooling knowledge and genetic material on every crop grown on the planet, in addition to research on livestock breeding, plant and animal diseases, and cropping systems.

These scientists know what is happening because they are making it happen. And what they make happen has yet another dimension of great, but often overlooked, importance. The new biotechnology, unlike mechanical technology, does not demand the substitution of capital for labor. Critchfield reports from the field: "Large scale experience in Asia during the 1970s shows that it is more labor intensive, not less."

Let me add to Critchfield's deeply meaningful observations my own vision of the enormous potential that agriculture holds for all of us on this planet. Not long ago an interesting article appeared in the *New York Times*, written by the eminent scientist and ecologist, Dr. Rene Dubos, while he was a professor at Rockefeller University. Dr. Dubos pointed out that only about half of the usable land in the world today is actually being used. Only half!

To illustrate what can be done, not only with this empty space crying out for action but even beyond it, he cites two areas in the world where usable land that historically did not exist has literally been created and is now notably productive.

One is the area around Brasilia, the capital of Brazil. Built 50 miles into the hinterlands twenty years ago, Brasilia today is a city of a couple of million people. The area surrounding it, millions of acres, was scrub forestland, totally unproductive. Today that land is intensively cultivated and profitably so. There are probably 400 million acres of potentially productive land in Brazil, more than all the land under cultivation in the United States.

On the other side of the world, in Australia, is an area that was 90 miles of desert but has, in a comparable way, with the addition of soil nutrients and other available technologies, also become highly productive.

In addition, there are hundreds of millions of acres in Africa that have the potential to become equally productive. Sudan alone has as much land not under the plow as the land used for agricultural production in the United States. The problem is that there are no railroads, no storage, no people, and no know-how. But the potential is there.

As a matter of fact, on the subject of combining the potential of land not in use and the agricultural technology that exists and is not used, Roger Lavell, an eminent American scientist, wrote recently in *Scientific American:* "If the level of technology and resources were applied to land around the world and employed at levels comparable to the usage of a typical Iowa corn farmer in the U.S., enough food could be produced to sustain 38–40 million people."

Given the cutting-edge technology we now have, plus the demonstrated productivity of the family farm, what can be done in this vital area is almost commensurate with what needs to be done. The needs are clear and staggering. The Presidential Commission on World Hunger, constituted in the fall of 1979, defined these needs in starkly realistic terms:

(1) Approximately 25 percent of the world's population are hungry or undernourished;

(2) Malnutrition affects more than 500 million persons;

(3) Twelve to 13 million small children die each year, the majority from malnutrition-associated causes;

(4) Approximately one out of three children born into the world will die before reaching the age of five, mostly from malnutrition-related causes;

(5) Between fifty and one hundred thousand children throughout the world become blind every year due to vitamin A deficiency;

(6) The majority of hungry people exist in well-defined geographic areas, concentrated on the Indian subcontinent, Southeast Asia, and sub-Saharan Africa, with pockets in the Middle East and Latin America; and

(7) Hunger is a major health problem for some 500 million individuals, an ethical, moral, and human rights problem for the rest of the world, and a world order problem if the alarming spread of hunger is allowed to continue.

Fortunately we do not have to head into that dark night. Alternatives exist. Positive solutions are possible. And the key to them is the family farm.

It is estimated—obviously a rough estimate—that there exist about 1 billion farm families in developing countries around the world, owning and working less than 5 hectares of land each. If these 1 billion farm families were helped to increase their net income by only $100 a year, the local impact would be enormous. Not only would their own lives and the lives of their families and communities improve measurably, but the additional purchasing power would also provide a tremendous stimulus to the economies of their villages and their countries.

Further, the impact on the growth and expansion of the world economy would be significant. These 1 billion farmers constitute a gigantic new market. Many of the problems the global economy struggles with today would find a solution that is both quick and sound. The world economy would surge dramatically. It would spell the end of the stagflation that has haunted us for the past decade. And it would lay a foundation for a sane and sustainable global economic order for all.

Another important result would be to reverse the massive migration of impoverished people, from the countryside to horrible, putrid city slums, that is taking place all over the world.

The vital question then becomes how the miraculous dynamics of the family farm can be sustained at home and propagated abroad. I am convinced that it requires a working partnership between the private and public sectors, shaped to the social, political, and cultural norms of the respective societies.

Reviewing agricultural production worldwide, two facts seem incontrovertible. One is that large production units and collectivism as a social and economic structure usually do not work well. The latest example of this is in the German Democratic Republic (G.D.R.), where the regime merged eight hundred thousand farming units, mostly family farms, into four thousand "agricultural factories" averaging 5,000 hectares each. This was done in 1955, with the result that today the G.D.R. imports up to 4 million tons of grain a year, mainly from the United States, since the U.S.S.R. has none to spare. The imports eat up 20 percent of East Germany's hard currency earnings and prompted G.D.R. chairman Erich Honecker to declare, in July 1982: "Today, one can compare the grain problem with the oil problem in terms of priority."

The second incontrovertible fact seems to be that something about the agricultural producer and his or her relation to the land is sui generis. Still the farmer and the land, however strong the bond between them, do not constitute an economic or social island. Fair market conditions, access to technology, credit, the appropriate chemical imports, the required physical infrastructure—in which government attitudes and policies inevitably play a role—are part of the system in which the individual producer can get the desired results. Where such a system is in place, where the combination of access to supplies and to the market exist, and where government policies recognize the importance of stable and reasonable prices, the individual producer, whose reward is clearly the product of one's own effort, has demonstrated initiative and creativity that have delivered results unmatched by any other approach.

This is true not only in the United States, but also in places with cultures and traditions as different as Taiwan, South Korea, and Israel. In each case, however, the basic components of success were the same: a private sector, encouraged by sensitive and effective government support, to stimulate productivity.

The question then becomes, how can the success story of the American family farm be "exported?" How can smallholders in the developing countries, families that cultivate 1–5 hectares (which, for the present, is a working definition of the family farm in these countries), be organized and energized to increase their productivity?

The answer is a novel hybrid that I have seen successfully introduced over the past decade in Latin America, Asia, and Africa. The hybrid I refer to is not a generic one; it is structural. It is, in fact, an integrated system in which a corporate core serves to move individual farmers from subsistence agriculture into the market economy.

In this system, private-sector companies, processors, and marketers of foodstuffs and industrial crops develop an integrated operation in areas of potential productivity. They reach agreement with small producers, guaranteeing a market at a fair price and providing credit, technology, inputs such as fertilizers, herbicides, and seeds, assistance in soil preparation, harvesting, and storage, and, finally, services in moving the product to processing and market. In some parts of the world, where land is abundant, farmers who participate in such a scheme develop the know-how to move out of their miniplots and learn to manage larger tracts of land, graduating into larger, family-size farms. This is not a process that can take place overnight. It requires long-term planning, infrastructure in place, and dependable government support so that investments made by the private sector and responsibility carried forward are protected for the long haul. If it is to succeed, it requires, in addition, the involvement and support of the entire rural community.

The key is a holistic approach, with a broad involvement of people, particularly women, who do an estimated 78 percent of the farming in most developing countries and whose willingness and capacity to make necessary changes has been demonstrated time and again when they have been properly approached and mobilized. Once increased production brings money into the pockets of small producers, production techniques spread rapidly throughout the community, stimulating a host of related economic activities, which in turn provide jobs for the landless and build new markets. The process can multiply wealth rapidly, creating a winning situation with four dimensions:

(1) A substantial increase in the living standard of small farms;

(2) An important contribution to the sound development of the host country;

(3) A profitable undertaking for the core company; and

(4) An input into meeting the basic human needs for nutrition around the world.

Global experience with this hybrid makes it possible to produce a set of guidelines that can constitute a framework for action combining the proven potential of the family farm with the demonstrated dynamic of a corporate core.

In the operational area, to achieve a successful symbiosis between a corporate core and a network of smallholder farmers, the following conditions are mandatory:

(1) A firm, clear agreement between the family farmers and the company. Under this agreement, the farm family must commit itself to adopt the company's techniques and practices to grow the product. They must commit themselves as well to prompt harvesting and delivery to the processing facility to make possible a continuous flow of product to the processing facility. The company, for its part, must contract for the product at a fair and equitable price level and make a dependable commitment to provide credit, inputs, and technical assistance. The details of such agreements inevi-

tably vary, depending on crop, conditions, country, and culture, but the contract must conform as far as possible to local practices and customs.

(2) An efficient and specialized advisory service that constantly reviews the training and supervision of the farmers, as well as the corporate staff, in the production, processing, and marketing facets of the operation. Such an advisory service can also interpret the organization to the community and can communicate to all parties the importance of performance and the advantages that will result to participants in the enterprise from performance. Conversely, it can advise the company on people and community problems that may arise.

(3) The company's visible responsibility for efficient management of the operation, from soil preparation to marketing of the final product. Management is critical and, historically, has been the most serious shortfall in carrying such satellite farming programs forward successfully. Companies must make top-level managers available to run these enterprises.

(4) A comprehensive research facility that can explore the latest technology and instruct and assist farmers in the application of the best production practices. This is a vital ingredient in boosting both farmer income and corporate responsibility.

In the systemic area, there are also four important conditions:

(1) Market orientation, the most important systemic element for success. The needs of the market must be rigorously identified and measured before a project is launched. There are many distressing examples of decision makers concentrating on production capacity without identifying and defining the market. A project will not work if the cart gets before the horse, which is what happens when production takes priority over the market.

(2) Overall management in the hands of a single authority, including allocation and coordination of all aspects of production, processing, and marketing.

(3) Long-term orientation of all participants. For the company, this means a stretching out of profit expectations; for the farmer, it means accepting instruction and guidance over a protracted period.

(4) A balanced approach to local culture and traditions, often the crux of a successful operation. Management must recognize and address this dimension from the outset. Failure to do so will haunt the enterprise and can threaten its viability in the long run.

In the policy area, aid programs in industrialized countries that focus on agriculture should secure maximum participation from the private sector to ensure the most dynamic approach and the most effective results. A system of family farms grouped around a corporate core has great potential. The experience of companies that have successfully implemented this system could be made available to other firms to enlist their interest and abbreviate their learning period.

Governments of industrialized countries with aid programs designed for the agricultural sector should approach agricultural and agribusiness companies with demonstrated records of know-how and performance. They must make clear to these companies that the government assigns high priority to effective agricultural undertakings in the developing world and is prepared to undergird this priority with credit facilities and perhaps also with insurance and other mechanisms that ameliorate the corporate risk in such long-term and often politically vulnerable undertakings. Specifically, the governments of industrialized countries should promise to use their best efforts to see that host governments honor their commitments to companies prepared to take the risk. In the United States, the Bureau of Private Enterprise in the Agency for International Development is giving serious consideration to providing this kind of support to companies prepared to launch agricultural undertakings based on the family farm system. Other industrialized countries should adopt the same policy.

In addition to mobilizing and supporting their own private-sector companies willing to undertake agricultural projects in developing countries, the industrialized nations should also support the host countries that welcome these enterprises. Such support could take the form of assistance to the host government for farm-to-market roads, irrigation, and social and educational services in the rural areas. It could include support for training in the agricultural sector at educational institutions, and perhaps even for on-site training provided by the companies under a special contract.

International institutions, particularly development banks, which have credit, prestige, and experience, should put their considerable muscle behind such undertakings. The World Bank, for example, can be a powerful force, with great influence on the host country in facilitating the necessary follow-through on commitments made and in resisting the inevitable political meddling that occurs in developing countries when real change takes place.

Host country policies are, of course, basic. Today, the political leadership in most of the developing countries recognizes that food production is a key to progress and that a healthy agricultural sector is basic to sound economic development. The recognition was long in coming and, in too many cases, the gap between rhetoric and action is still wide. It will be necessary to bridge this gap in developing countries in order to get companies with production and processing know-how and marketing expertise to commit themselves to the substantial risks involved in such agricultural enterprises, with all their complexities and long-term payouts.

There are four keys to understanding the full meaning and impact of agriculture, all lessons learned from the superb success record of the family farm in the United States:

(1) Agriculture is the key to economic development. No country, with the exception of a few city-states, has ever prospered and built a sound economy without a solid agricultural base.

(2) Agriculture is different from other economic sectors. The forces with which agriculture must contend and which it must mold and master are quite different from the forces affecting indus-

try. Agriculture is subject to outside, uncontrollable elements: weather, diseases, pests, to name a few. Also, farmers, like other raw-material producers, have a relatively weak bargaining position, falling short of the return that processors and marketers of raw materials get from the marketplace. Management in agriculture is difficult. It is much easier to manage and produce efficiently using 2,500 acres of land. This is why large-scale producing units are extremely difficult to operate efficiently and profitably. The family farm, with a landholding adequate to apply modern technology effectively, is the most productive size. The incentive that results when producers benefit directly from their efforts cannot be duplicated by large holdings, whether privately held, communal, cooperative, or state owned. Results from the factory-size organization of state farms and large collectives in the U.S.S.R. are dramatic demonstrations of how not to organize agriculture.

(3) Sound agricultural policies are difficult to develop and carry out. The time span required to put into place an appropriate land-people balance, to make credit and necessary inputs available to the grower, and to construct storage, processing, and marketing capacity, is longer than the usual time span of a political officeholder. In addition, carrying out a sound, meaningful agricultural policy calls for changes that, by their very nature, shake up traditional patterns and are fiercely resisted.

(4) A system whereby the producer on the soil benefits directly from his or her efforts is the single most important element in increasing productivity. In most places in the world, this means producer ownership and requires egalitarian land policies, adequately supported by the government. Taiwan, Japan, and Korea are examples of success where this principle has been applied.

Concentration on the family farm is the key to success, both in increasing productivity everywhere in the world and in creating a sociopolitical base for a society in which self-reliance, enterprise, and commitment to cohesive family relationships are important and enduring values.

Orville L. Freeman   140

THE CASE OF 3M

GORDON W. ENGDAHL

A corporate environment can be restrictive, with goals and performances set in advance. It can also allow substantial freedoms for its employees. My experience is based on an organizational structure and work climate that encourages initiative in each employee by providing both direction and freedom to work creatively.

The company I joined forty years ago as a research engineer was a little-known midwestern maker of sandpaper, clear adhesive tape, and little else. It had about six thousand employees and annual sales of $47 million. Operations were centered largely in Minnesota, with a few people in Wisconsin and Michigan. Sales were confined almost entirely to the United States, and the company had made no direct investments outside the country.

The firm was at that time about forty years old, having been incorporated just after the turn of the century as the Minnesota Mining and Manufacturing Company. The three Ms of the legal name included one misnomer: Mining had been a goal of the original founders, but all serious thought of mining dissolved when a deposit of supposedly valuable minerals proved worthless. It took ten years for the struggling young firm to achieve a measure of success as a sandpaper manufacturer. It was fourteen years before the initial investors reaped their first dividend, six cents a share in 1916.

When I joined the company in 1943, its publicly owned stock was still not listed on any major exchange. Few would have encouraged a newly graduated chemical engineer to leave Illinois and launch his business career with 3M in Minnesota, as I did. In the forty years since then—until my retirement in 1983 as 3M vice-president for human resources—I have seen many changes.

Instead of six thousand employees, 3M now has close to eighty-six thousand. They are located in more than thirty states and fifty countries. Instead of $47 million in annual sales, 3M now has close to $7 billion a year in sales. The company's stock is not only listed on the New York Stock Exchange, but it has also become a component of the most widely watched business barometer of all: the Dow Jones Industrial Average. A one-dollar share of 1943 3M stock would today be worth about $160.

Instead of serving only a few markets with a narrow range of products and technologies, 3M is one of the most broadly based and highly diversified technology companies in the world. It is a company that has grown at least twice as fast as the gross national product. Each year, 20–25 percent of sales result from products or services that were new in the previous five years.

Relating some of this history is essential if I am to link the 3M story to our theme—high technology and human freedom. I am convinced that a good organizational environment for industrial innovation is as much a product of heritage as it is of hierarchy. In the early days of 3M, as it happens, the heritage and the hierarchy came together in the person of William L. McKnight, long-time leader of the company and in many important ways the architect of 3M's early growth. He deserves much of the credit for the work environment I encountered when I first came to 3M. It was a company of small work groups and a personal touch in its employee relations, a company where each individual was looked upon as a valuable resource, and a company where management believed that nothing much happens in the workplace without strong personal motivation. This spirit prevailed as 3M grew and diversified. It is the secret of 3M's success over the years.

McKnight was not a technical genius; his specialty was finance. As 3M's technologies and markets expanded, he knew instinctively that it was necessary to bet on the people of the company. (Interestingly enough, he was also known to bet on horses. One of his prize possessions in later years was an all-time great thoroughbred, Dr. Fager.)

McKnight once told his 3M colleagues, "As our business grows, it becomes increasingly necessary to delegate responsibilty and to encourage men and women to exercise their initiative. This requires considerable tolerance. Those to whom we delegate authority and responsibility, if they are good people, are going to want to do their jobs in their own way. These are characteristics we want, and people should be encouraged as long as their way conforms to our general pattern of operations.

"Mistakes will be made," he said, "but if a person is essentially right, the mistakes he or she makes are not as serious in the long run as the mistakes management will make if it is dictatorial and undertakes to tell those under its authority exactly how they must do their jobs."

He added, "Management kills initiative if it is destructively critical when mistakes are made, and it is essential that we have many people with initiative if we are to continue to grow."

McKnight's willingness to bet on people, to delegate authority, and to persevere in the face of occasional failures has remained part of the 3M heritage. I recall that, at one point early in my 3M career, the company had made a massive investment in fluorochemicals. Dozens of chemists had been hired, and extensive research had been conducted. Nevertheless, the project seemed nowhere near successful commercialization. As chairman of the board, McKnight faced considerable pressure to kill the project and release the highly paid scientists. Instead he called in each of the forty researchers on the program and interviewed them personally, asking them questions and looking into their eyes to gauge for himself their confidence in the project.

He decided to continue the venture, not because he understood the technology involved but rather because of his faith in the people working on the project. As a result, 3M today has a highly successful business in Scotchgard fabric treatments and related fluorochemical products. This particular 3M spirit of faith remains unchanged.

There have been, of course, major organizational and physical changes as the company grew to its present size. For example, before the late 1940s, all of the company's executives participated in the development and sale of each product line. Responsibility for profits was widely dispersed throughout the entire organization, but efficient management under the traditional pyramid structure was becoming difficult. The company was in danger of strangling on its own growth.

Operations were divided into eight separate divisions, each with a general manager having full authority and responsibility for research and development, manufacturing, and sales. With this type of structure, new divisions could be created as necessary without greatly increasing the burden on top management. In many important ways, 3M remained a single integrated and interrelated business organization. Some companies carry a vertical organization, placing all staff services under divisional control. 3M remained strongly centralized in a few core functions. Thomas J. Peters and Robert H. Waterman, Jr., the authors of *In Search of Excellence* (Harper & Row, 1984) call this "operating with simultaneous loose-tight properties."

These core values at 3M include sound financial practice, quality engineering, and equitable human resource policies. Each centralized function is responsible to a corporate vice-president. A manager from each function is assigned to every division operating committee to ensure consistent practice throughout the company.

Still, 3M's vertical organization did not fully extend to staff services. For many years, the human resource values of the company were unwritten and transmitted to new generations of management largely by word of mouth. More recently, the previously uncodified "3M way" was defined on paper as a set of human resource principles. Now we have a basic personnel charter, strongly influenced by the current chief executive, Lewis W. Lehr.

These principles state that "the people of 3M are the company's most valuable resource. They are the primary means by which 3M goals and objectives will be attained." It goes on to elaborate on an organizational structure and work climate that respects the dignity and worth of individuals, encourages the initiative of each employee, challenges individual capabilities, and provides equal opportunity. These principles are posted at 3M locations throughout the world—not in the manager's office, but out in the open where everyone can see them because, as Lew Lehr says, "we must be held accountable by our employees."

Employee initiative is encouraged by the development of smaller units that provide greater freedom of operation. One of our previous chief executives said, "Over the years, we have discovered that when a division reaches a certain size, it has a tendency to spend too much of its time on established products and markets, and a lesser amount on new products and businesses."

New management teams are needed, he added, when the new businesses begin to give those involved an opportunity to identify with the new venture and become more important to 3M. Under this approach, the new units begin to grow at a faster rate than the company as a whole. The established divisions then are inspired to find other new products and markets that help meet 3M's growth objectives. It is a process of renewal.

This is the way magnetic recording materials, a spinoff of electrical products, grew to become first a division by itself and then a group of divisions. It is the way a copying machine project grew to become an office equipment division. And it is the way a new venture in printing products eventually became an entire graphic arts group of divisions.

Lew Lehr is a prime example of how this system works. While a customer service engineer for 3M's tape products, he became interested in potential medical applications for the company's tape technology. Without neglecting his regular duties, Lehr became instrumental in the development of surgical drapes and special medical tapes for patient comfort. He had a number of false starts and more than a few disappointments, but he kept going and finally established a medical products division. This division had just a few million dollars of sales in the early 1960s. Fifteen years later, his fledgling venture had grown to become a half-billion-dollar-a-year business. Today, that group includes medical, surgical, dental, orthopedic, and pharmaceutical businesses.

This divide-and-grow philosophy has led one Massachusetts Institute of Technology professor to credit 3M with "the most consistently effective performance with internal ventures I know of." Writing in the *Harvard Business Review* in 1980, management professor Edward B. Roberts noted that: "More than most other major corporations, 3M has thoroughly organized itself to encourage and support internal ventures. . . . From top to bottom, 3M's management provides active, spirited encouragement for new venture generation."

At 3M, each division is held accountable for achieving growth sales, but within divisions there can be smaller business development units planning new segments and operating with similar disciplines at a lower level. These development teams are an extension of the division general manager's office. They explore the future as a closely knit team and operate with what Dr. William Ouchi's *Theory Z* (Addison-Wesley, 1971) calls the "creative dynamics of consensus decision making."

Despite 3M's experience, there is no perfect organizational

model or ideal business climate that guarantees similar successes. There are times when employees must be free and willing to "fight the system" in the best interests of the company. There are dozens of anecdotes to support this thesis. For example, some years ago there was a laboratory worker on our payroll who was fired, but still kept coming in to the lab to work on his pet project. With the persistence of his efforts and his eventual rehiring, the project became a division. The persistent employee ultimately retired as the vice-president of this very successful operation.

Another young lab worker was experimenting with tiny glass beads, more a novelty than a product. He was told to get back to his regular work. He did, but fortunately he also returned to his bead project after normal working hours. Many nights, he burned the midnight oil. Today, those tiny beads are on reflective road and bridge safety signs all over the world. Just a few years ago, he and his wife attended an Academy Awards ceremony where he received an Oscar for a bead-based front screen projection system for moviemakers.

The first of our Scotch-brand tapes, back in the 1920s, was developed in much the same way by a technician who was concerned about a customer problem, the two-tone painting of automobiles. This was shortly after a great American innovator offered the public any color car they wanted, provided it was black. Again, the 3M innovator continued to tinker with various adhesive and backing agents. The result was masking tape; a new industry was born.

We keep these stories alive and tell them often, so all our employees are encouraged by the innovative tradition of 3M. The masking tape episode created a certain tolerance for tinkerers by 3M management and a pattern of further experimentation and innovation that has led us to the broadly based, diversified position we have in world markets today.

The point of these anecdotes is that industrial innovation requires the right people in the right climate. Management does have a great deal to do with selecting and assigning people. And management, to a large measure, controls the climate or environment by the way it allocates resources and apportions psychological and financial incentives and rewards. The environment has to be a challenging one, for the best and the hardest work is done in a spirit of adventure and challenge.

Part of that environment at our company is a collection of five thousand technical people in almost fifty different research laboratories. Another part of the environment is a massive, continuing, and fairly formal effort to promote cross-communication between technical innovators. Through an internal organization called the Technical Forum, with more than two dozen chapters and committees, our technical people from different labs are in continuing dialogue with each other. This helps all of us learn from the mistakes and failures that only one of us may have experienced. We accept mistakes as a normal part of running a business and an essential byproduct of industrial innovation, but we expect our mistakes to have originality. We can afford almost any mistake once.

There is no formula or recipe for building this kind of environment. There are, however, practices and policies that contribute to it. For example, we have an informal practice of allowing research scientists the freedom to devote 15 percent of their time to unassigned personal research pursuits. They use company equipment and facilities to explore wherever their creativity leads them.

Our management has also created a structure and a personnel practice that allows an individual to enjoy a series of different careers without leaving the company. I, for instance, was given the opportunity to move from the technical area to manufacturing, to new business development, to general management, and finally to human resources.

An innovator who is so inclined can become an entrepreneur who uses his or her development to build a business. He or she may have the option, however, to progress on the technical side of a "dual ladder" to corporate scientist rank, which is the equivalent of senior technical management. We do not hire someone for a project and view that person as just another part in the production process. Instead, 3M hires a person for a career and then trains him or her for a lifetime of contributions. It is a corporate attitude that works to encourage innovation. As W. L. McKnight said, when reviewing his sixty-five-year relationship with 3M, "To continue our progress and service to America and the world, we need a healthy appreciation of those who exercise the free man's option for excellence, permitting the creation of something for all of us, enriching lives with new ideas and products."

ORGANIZATION SIZE, EFFECTIVENESS, AND HUMAN VALUES

LEONARD R. SAYLES

One of the proud inventions of humankind has been the large organization. The ability of a small group or a single leader to control and direct the energies of thousands or hundreds of thousands is considered an extraordinary accomplishment.

It has been asserted that such size has numerous advantages. Large projects not otherwise possible get completed, like pyramids and space stations. Economies of scale are possible—meaning it becomes worthwhile to design and utilize costly machinery, specialized professional talent and departments, and complex routines because the cost of these can be spread over multiple and frequent uses. Large organizations also economize on the scarcity of talented leaders. The abilities, insights, and visions of a single Edwin Land or Thomas Watson or George Eastman are implemented on a massive scale because their organizations will mobilize the combined energies of thousands of others who follow and defer. Public postal systems and private worldwide distribution networks operate efficiently because large organizations have been created.

Such massive organizations are possible because of a number of social inventions and certain human characteristics. As Herbert Simon argued persuasively, hierarchy, that one particular social convention, is an extraordinary innovation. Hierarchies basically allow direction to proceed through a number of levels and linkages that are not serially related. That is, where there is a flaw— incompetence, defection, or some other disobedience or failure— the system does not fail, because the hierarchy has created the equivalent of watertight compartments. Although Division A may be a disaster, Divisions B, C, and D can continue to function and the departments under them will continue to receive organizational nourishment even though A is out of action. Hierarchies also work because no leader could control thousands directly but must use intermediaries, who in turn use other intermediaries. These characteristics are the essence of hierarchy.

There is little question that one can control large numbers of human beings by small numbers, just as one can use a semiconductor transmitting an extraordinarily small amount of current to control high-energy systems. Hierarchies do work. The Catholic church, traditional armies, and many business organizations represent large hierarchies and often relative efficiency.

We also know that human beings will follow leaders who represent admired values, physical security, or potential psychic or monetary rewards. Crusaders ransacked the Holy Land with the promise of salvation, excitement, and booty; automobile assembly-line workers tolerate miserable jobs because they pay well. Rewards and punishments do work when leaders seek to gain dutiful followers. Human beings apparently can learn quite readily to be responsive to leaders, even those they rarely know personally.

Recently, American business has come under a barrage of criticism for its failure to maintain competitiveness, particularly with the Japanese. What one sees is that large size has enabled many organizations to appear successful (efficient, profitable, even innovative) when they in fact have not been. Large size enables organizations to engage in a variety of financial activities (particularly acquisitions) that for some period can give the appearance of growth and dynamism. Further, for short periods, size in relation to the market, including distribution facilities and advertising budgets, allows reasonable revenue growth even in the face of internal inefficiencies and lack of innovation.

It has come as an unpleasant revelation to many that well-known, well-established firms in some of America's most basic industries were backward in their technology, relatively inefficient in processing goods and utilizing inventories, and consistently mediocre in the quality of their products. In part by sheer size, by the cover-up provided by inflation (which during the 1970s papered over many mistakes) and by growing markets, these firms looked successful to the outside world—shareholders and citizens alike. With less buoyant markets, more stable prices (which did not allow continuous price rises to cover inflated costs), and keen world-class competition, the reality became apparent: these were modern-day dinosaurs, clumsy and vulnerable.

Many economies of scale derived from bigness turn out to be diseconomies. Ford built a well-automated, massive factory in the 1970s whose sole product was V–8 engines. There was no flexibility or adaptability. The huge investments in open-hearth steel mills by Bethlehem and U.S. Steel represented the best of a technology that was fast becoming obsolete.

With technology changing as fast as it does, tying manufacturing methods to an inflexible, heavily capitalized facility can produce short-run savings but long-run disaster. In the U.S. steel industry, for example, much smaller, geographically dispersed facilities using a newer closed-cycle technology built around the basic oxygen furnace maintained profitability even against subsidized foreign competition. Their big brethren have accumulated heavy losses in the meantime.

Smaller size is also associated with a higher degree of contracting out. Options are kept open to shift suppliers (and technologies) with minimal commitments when considerable portions of manu-facturing requirements are contracted out. This policy contrasts sharply with the now-devalued policy of complete vertical integra-tion. Perhaps the most extreme and therefore usefully illustrative example of the destructiveness of that policy was Ford's efforts to control everything related to automobile production. Ford built its own "Rouge" steel mill and even acquired rubber plantations—all highly inefficient. The coal and iron mines, coke plants, and ship-ping and port facilities of the integrated steel companies have turned out to be albatrosses.

Where there is a rigid technology and a fixed product line, and where management's primary aim is to exploit existing routines to the utmost, with little or no room for adaptiveness or employee initiative, large fixed-purpose facilities and organizations may work reasonably well. For some years it worked in automobile manufac-ture; there were almost no real technological improvements in the basic engine of the U.S. car after the automatic transmission came in the 1950s. In fact, there was overt hostility to using discoveries like fuel injection, which languished for more than a decade after it had been perfected. But car makers could deliver bigger, more luxurious, and more powerful automobiles at reduced costs per pound or per horsepower. Unfortunately, as we know too well, the ability to do the wrong thing better and better is not exactly functional.

These large bureaucratic organizations work on the basis of strict rules, accountability, and insistence on following the chain of com-mand. Most authority rests firmly at the top of what is a real pyra-mid; little discretion is delegated to lower levels, and little initiative is expected or given.

Many of these errors and self-deceptions of our large organiza-tions grew out of the failure to employ individuals effectively. Be-cause there was little value placed on information from those clos-est to operations or to the problem, there was a tendency to make plans and decisions based on pure extrapolations of the past (e.g., the market for large U.S. cars would grow indefinitely with population growth) or arbitrary presumptions necessary to maintain status (messengers with bad news are still not welcome after all these hundreds of years).

Large, impersonal organizations with fragmented, diffuse responsibility chains also provide fertile ground for illicit, antisocial decisions. Increasingly impersonal decision making allows "passing the buck," "cooking the books," or ignoring responsibilities. (In fairness, it must also be pointed out that large bureaucracies in the United States are less tightly "locked" than the casual observer might think, and it is quite possible for well-motivated and intelligent managers and professionals to move deftly within the interstices of such structures to innovate and undertake creative acts.) At lower levels, at least until recently, the tendency has been to minimize discretion and even to infantilize workers by extreme divisions of labor that destroy the ability to take initiative, improvise, or use judgment.

Fortunately, this kind of foolishness, the product the basic conceptual errors of the early scientific-management movement, is being countered. Business organizations are discovering the high cost to both motivation and coordination of minutely divided jobs and of work that does not demand any intellectual effort.

For workers and managers alike, the traditional large organizations provided little real freedom because there was no responsibility. Managers had extended hierarchical lines to those who had final responsibility, and workers had narrow, stultifying tasks. Both abdicated real responsibility and, in turn, had none of the joys or growth potential inherent in taking responsibility for accomplishments or innovation.

The extremes of specialization that have been favored in large organizations also discourage solidarity at both worker and managerial levels. Countless studies in industry show fruitless intergroup conflicts and interlevel frictions.

The division of labor that Adam Smith regarded (legitimately at the time) as the source of enormous productivity improvement also has the potential for creating high-cost operations. Field studies show that increased specialization within management (in contrast to the worker level that Smith described) can lead to great inefficiency.

The problem is twofold. More specialists require more coordination. Secondly, each specialist has a tendency to elaborate the task given and thereby increase the total amount of effort required of other managers and professionals.

Coordination is not a free good. Within smaller groups, individuals contribute a great deal of the organizational "sinews" even without formal training, direction, or compensation. This is the well-known informal organization, in which styles of give-and-take evolve through trial and error and tend to be self-maintaining and to cause little upset or interruption. It works because the members of the group want a reasonably predictable, stress-free work life (which requires self-maintaining, reciprocal exchanges in coordination) and because they are able to have sufficiently frequent contact to develop common loyalties and identifications. These "motivate" or support coordinative responsibility.

Among strangers and, most frequently, between members of noninteracting groups, there is a tendency for the reverse to occur. Mutual responsiveness is costly and is therefore avoided as coordination is neglected. What are called misunderstandings, conflicts, and breakdowns are most often reactions of one group to requests by another for some resource or some change in priority or accommodation. The dynamics of the organization discourage granting the request responsively. To defer to new initiatives with any regularity assures one of lower status, which can lead to a loss of perquisites and power. Even more costly, the dynamics of the interacting parties are likely to disrupt the routines that are the source of internal harmony and stability within the small system.

Workers now recognize that specialization by craft means that no finished work can be done until all of the necessary artisans, to repair a machine or hang a door, for example, have been coordinated in time and space—no simple task. In contrast, a non-specialized artisan, who knows the whole machine or who can cope with a whole door (and jamb and lock and closer), waits for no one and can do the job more expeditiously.

Within management, the conflicts over deference and who should do what, when, and how are complicated by the ability of the incumbent in any job to elaborate his or her function in a way that provides less deference to others and commands more deference from others. When large numbers of managers "upgrade" their tasks this way, the amount of managerial time required in the system to do the managerial work tends to increase, probably exponentially.

The result is a spiral of increasing coordination efforts leading to heavier managerial workloads and to the need for more specialists to deal with coordination breakdowns and more managers to deal with the increasing number of personnel. In effect, the large, more specialized organizations start to grow quite independently of the volume of real work being processed and become increasingly less efficient.

The smaller organization with less specialization and more close, accommodating, interrole work relationships produces no such dynamic. Quite the reverse: individuals discover that by being responsive to others they get more aid in return and that by learning to improvise to cope with unanticipated events they can prevent crises that are stressful and painful.

In the large organization, improvisation and the crossing of formal job boundaries is much more likely to be a punishing experience; arguments ensue over "turf" and legalities.

Many of the recent demands for "give backs" in collective bargaining are in relation to an excessive number of "watertight" job compartments that not only make day-to-day coordination more costly (e.g., if an employee cannot pick up a fallen piece of work because that is janitorial work) but also handicap transfers as workloads change. Although such job compartmentalization is blamed on unions, which surely learned how to manipulate job descriptions and classifications to their advantage, the lessons were first taught by managers following the precepts of scientific management: divide work as finely as possible, prescribe minutely what the employee is supposed to do, train people only for that one, highly routinized task, and allow no personal judgment. This is a formula for maximizing the number of workers and the amount of supervision that will be required. One extreme case is indicative:

A large hospital conscious of both the cost and lack of hygiene resulting from bed linens being stacked in corridors and carted through halls and down elevators to the laundry constructed chutes in all patient areas. However, no existing job description called for "pushing dirty laundry down laundry chute," and the union insisted that new employees would have to be hired to do that newly added task.

Large organizations typically operate on the presumption that work can be accomplished by meticulously designing plans and procedures that specify who does what and how. Various rules, supervisors, and training programs are all used to make sure that these a priori plans are followed meticulously.

The best, although macabre, examples of the folly of this presumption occur in the military. Barbara Tuchman, in her *Guns of August*, best documents for World War I the follies of both the German and French armies, who proceeded to fight battles as prescribed in pre-1914 plans drawn up by their respective general staffs. Although the actual battle situations warranted quite different strategies, their respective commands insisted that their troops follow these long-since-outdated and even self-destructive plans.

World War II showed little new learning. Our command at Pearl Harbor stuck rigidly to its rather casual plans for mobilization and defense in spite of repeated warnings from Washington that the Japanese were engaged in a series of potentially threatening activities. One of the most devastating and costly defeats our armies suffered at the hands of the Germans, at Arnheim in the Netherlands, came about through the unwillingness of Allied commanders to modify their attack plans in the light of new information concerning the buildup of German defenses in that area.

Although there has been much discussion of the enormous advantages gained by a fighting force using semiautonomous units able to make real-time decisions in light of immediate battle conditions—witness the Israeli successes against vastly larger Arab forces—the military has been loath to allow this. The newspapers reported that the U.S. landings at Grenada in November 1983 were unique because they allowed commanders on the scene to make real-time decisions. In contrast, our abortive efforts to rescue American hostages in Iran were directed from Washington through a number of hierarchical levels.

More decentralization, more democracy, and greater flexibility have begun to infiltrate the military, not as a result of changed attitudes toward what are appropriate leadership styles but to reflect changes in technology. Mobile, high-firepower units composed of highly trained experts require autonomy if their skill and destructive powers are to be best utilized. Structure is driven by technology, not changes in popular attitudes toward administrative styles.

Larger organizations inevitably encourage conservatism. Although many may try to allow culture to differ among units with strongly divergent tasks and environments, inevitably the existence of a common headquarters induces or seduces pressures toward uniformity.

Since organizations fear, with some legitimacy, adverse coercive comparisons (what is sometimes called "whip sawing"), they seek to provide universal recruiting, selection, compensation, and even promotion policies—even though the general rule may be nonsensical in a specific case.

Inevitably the values of the top of the hierarchy permeate the rest of the organization. Attitudes toward what are sensible endeavors or new pursuits, what is fact and what is fancy, get broad acceptance because those with the highest status and substantial powers to reward and punish have these values. They, in turn, utilize symbols to highlight what they value or devalue.

In part, large organizations operate on the basis of predictable routines and outcomes, and great effort is expended to avoid surprises and to reduce uncertainty. This can lead to standardization at the expense of innovation, the short-term view at the expense of the long-term perspective.

Regrettably, larger organizations are more prone to impersonality and emphasis on status distinctions by level and meticulously prescribed job descriptions. Smaller organizations, when well run, minimize separate facilities (e.g., parking and eating) and are much more likely to have loosely prescribed jobs that allow for the proper influence of personality and motivational differences on job responsibility. The able employee can take initiative and responsibility and gain more recognition, thus encouraging effective performance.

In theory, the large organization can find ways of providing motivation and job satisfaction. In practice, there is an obvious set of problems. Unless it is possible to convert a large organization into a federation of relatively small units, the larger organization is much more likely to have the following characteristics:

(1) Multiple layers of managerial hierarchy that separate the most important leaders from most of the followers and also move the most powerful away from the reality of operations—an emphasis on vertical communications to the exclusion of lateral;

(2) Greater difficulty in maintaining communications and solidarity;

(3) A large number of interdependent units, who view themselves as having separate objectives but who must coordinate;

(4) More emphasis on rigid plans, often outdated before they are implemented;

(5) More use of many rigid, narrow job classifications, complicating coordination and demoralizing those with any interest in gaining a sense of accomplishment from finished work; and

(6) More power games, status ploys, and situations in which means are elaborated at the expense of ends.

The new technologies demand a far different type of organization. Short product life cycles, talented professionals who require autonomy, and the need for constant adaptability and innovation are the situational demands that command small-scale operations. Large, ponderous, monolithic systems cannot maintain the pace of change or hold the often irascible experts who inevitably know more than their high-level superiors about what the next generation of equipment requires.

Motivation that leads to both productivity and inventiveness in problem solving is better in small groups. Direct and reasonably frequent interaction with the real boss and an ability to see the total job provides employees with substantial satisfaction. Entrepreneurial start-up situations, in which everyone has a direct and immediate sense of the goals and the progress being made, and a feeling that the boss knows and cares for them and comprehends their contribution, bring enthusiasm and accomplishment.

Small size also permits employees to know one another and to gain the "charge" that is derived from seeing others respond to their initiations. Enormous energy is released in a setting where people share an obvious common goal, where they complement and supplement each other in give-and-take.

The seemingly inexhaustible drive and stamina of small, self-contained project groups, who will work round the clock for a personally present leader and supportive colleagues, is well established. As in wartime, when buddies die for one another, workers and managers alike in the interactional "hot house" of a small, self-contained group can perform feats. Even families and personal comforts are ignored in this highly motivating setting. And it is especially significant that the responsive, synchronized interaction among employees and their trusted, supportive boss does the motivating—not the promise of great reward. Although, to be sure, the clarity of a shared goal and continuous and credible feedback are also important elements in the coterminous group and project.

Collaboration is thus encouraged by proximity, a sense of shared community, and, as both a cause and an effect, the opportunity for a high frequency of interaction. It is also encouraged by organizational acceptance of jobs with overlapping responsibilities, in contrast to the rubrics of large organizations with little, watertight boxes representing utterly separate spheres of responsibility.

It is rare for real innovations to be produced in the plans and thoughts of managers far removed from day-to-day operations, whether those operations are laboratories, factory floors, or computational facilities. Innovation requires that someone who is immersed in the intracacies of a problem and its setting have reasonable autonomy and resources to pursue original—that is, unorthodox and somewhat unpredictable—solutions without fear of punishment for deviation or failure. The deviation is inevitable, and failure is always likely.

This presumes that real innovation follows the model of natural experiments, autonomous initiatives that occur as a result of a good mind relating to problems and opportunities. This is the pattern associated with entrepreneurs who build an organization to implement their unqiue vision and support it with enormous personal drive. It is also the model one sees at companies that encourage venture-minded professionals to strike out on their own, but with corporate support.

Innovation is inevitably the product of a small group or an inspired individual, because so many trade-offs among half-known facts and unstated premises have to be made and a wide variety of facts, opinions, and positions gathered and interrelated and "parsed." The mere quantity of information that is part of the process cannot be handled in extended networks or in serial contacts. There is backing and filling and circling and false starting.

Taking at face value the oft-stated generalization that every "relay" (linkage) in a communication net may halve the information transmitted and double the noise, it becomes difficult to conceive of many "leaps forward" being made through large organizations. And those who try soon learn that they must establish a smaller working group of special individuals who can interact with high frequency, exchange information, and make trade-offs over the full range of issues, functions, and dimensions that make up the problem or opportunity. The much-praised Lockheed "skunk works"—the isolated, small, informal workplace encompassing all the specialists—performed technological breakthroughs the same way we have come to expect from small university clusters or from the great laboratories of Bell or Cambridge.

Even IBM recently tried with substantial success the technique of isolating a small group of engineers and giving them a self-contained assignment. The extraordinary success of the IBM personal computer is due apparently to the rapidity and effectiveness with which this autonomous group designed the new computer, in part by violating well-established traditions and practices.

Some of the most critical attributes of work that contribute to the combination of high employee motivation and productivity have been observed in what is called *continuous process technology*, where no innovation is required. The most successful of these attributes (in terms of human and business values) occur in chemical processing plants, where one finds, based on suggestions made by Robert Blauner in *Alienation and Freedom* (University of Chicago Press, 1967), an almost ideal job design:

(1) A relatively small group of employees (ten to two hundred) are solely responsible for the total operation of a processing unit and able to see the impact of their efforts, the technical interrelationships of all the functions, and the final product.

(2) A set of jobs call for intragroup cooperation and social solidarity, and the sum of all the work required is coterminous with a work group, the members of which can communicate easily with one another.

(3) Immediate supervision is provided by a group leader who

is both a manager and a member of the work groups, what used to be called a "straw boss" or working supervisor. There is no major status gap between manager and employee.

(4) Employees can pace themselves, and in fact, group decisions are necessary as to the order in which maintenance jobs are done and when to take work breaks.

(5) The jobs in the group arrange themselves in a functional hierarchy, and employees learn more skilled tasks on the job. With any degree of motivation, promotion is ensured to more skilled tasks.

(6) Higher productivity results from groups working as groups, rather than from the summation of individual effort. Further, individual work is often more isolating and more boring (since it involves more repetition and an absence of interaction). The group takes responsibility for finely tuned maintenance, both because it is part of their responsibility and also because they actually work less hard when the equipment functions perfectly (in a self-maintaining mode). Thus managerial efficiency goals and work goals of a "good job" are almost synonymous, since working "smart" to keep the equipment maintained reduces total worker effort and maximizes total output. In sharp contrast, in other types of production, higher efficiency requires higher levels of input from employees and management and workers have legitimate conflicts over how much effort is "too much".

Recently, the *Wall Street Journal* described the extraordinary differences in morale and performance of a five-hundred-worker Alcan Aluminum Ltd. smelter in Quebec compared with its eighty-five-hundred-worker smelter. In a study of the National Aeronautics and Space Administration (*Managing Large Systems,* Harper, 1971), Margaret Chandler and I observed many small project groups that had adequate autonomy and behaved like small organizations with extraordinary élan and performance. Recently, Ford Motor Company has been experimenting with Japanese-style quality circles in a part of its axle and transmission division. Small groups of employees can stop the line where parts are defective and meet with vendors. Their criticisms and suggestions are taken seriously by middle management. In public statements, Ford management asserts that reject rates have dropped from 25 percent to 5 percent, and employee satisfaction and work motivation have soared.

All these examples have a number of structural components that relate to size: workers can see the whole, initiate changes directly to managers, interact with each other within the group, see directly and immediately the results of their efforts, and take pride in a successful output. In some way the interacting group is coterminus wth the work flow, and job boundaries are broad and sometimes fluid with lateral interactions predominating over hierarchical ones.

But how many managements are willing to accept the complexity of heterogeneous, relatively autonomous units? The parameters of scientific management still exert a stong pull; central control, consistency, and uniformity have strong appeal, and there is the tendency to revert to type, when experiments are tried, as soon as short-run results turn adverse.

Many major corporations have recognized that large size is a handicap, and they insist that all activities must be conducted within units containing no more than three or four hundred employees. William Whyte, undertaking a large-scale anthropological field research project in Peru, purposely designed an organization in which Peruvian institutions and individuals collaborating on the study would be independent contractors rather than part of a Cornell University-dominated, centralized research program. This gave the participants a greater sense of commitment since they were working for local institutions and superiors, physically and psychologically close. There was no sense of a domineering, wealthy, North American "boss," although the major direction of the project was determined by Cornell.

At some future time, historians will note one of the great ironies of the post–World War II period. Americans by culture favor change, are quick to improvise, enjoy flouting conventions (at least somewhat) and, at their best, are unorthodox, irascible, and innova-tive. It has taken substantial effort to constrain if not destroy this culturally reinforced instinct for creativity. Unfortunately, large or-ganizations in our traditional mass-production industries have been successful in gaining lock-step conformity from large num-bers of their employees at a high cost in motivation and acceptance of change. Employees have sought outlets for their creative ener-gies and individualism, not by problem solving to improve organi-zational effectiveness but by a wide variety of techniques to frus-trate supervision and to conduct illicit games on the job and escape from work.

The new technologies are less likely to create a changed culture than they are to release the deep-seated belief that even though something works, it can be changed—and for the better. If it was good enough for parents and grandparents, it probably is not good enough for today.

We are talking about material things and not spiritual values when we talk about change. But there is a pleasant confluence between America's good fortune in believing in the individual, in not accepting that which is given or declared safe orthodoxy, and in challenging the conventional and the organizational requirements for an age of high technology.

With some historical perspective, one could argue that capitalism may finally attain some of its original promise with respect to indi-vidual freedom. Its early growth required leeway for individuals to challenge established practices, invest, start businesses, compete, and ignore "just" prices, guild restrictiveness, and the tenets of the immobile medieval world.

But for an extended period, this freedom and encouragement of in-dividual initiative was restricted to a small number of entrepreneurs and top-level managers. The capitalism of the last hundred years emphasized hierarchy, control and conformity, and relative rigidity. Profits came from large size, long runs of almost identical products, huge single-purpose equipment, and employee conformity.

For countries like the United States, that period may have ended. A relatively free world market and rapid industrialization in low-wage countries means that we are not competitive, and probably cannot be, for products that are highly standardized. The newer technologies and the increasingly short product life cycles often are associated with the opposite kind of organizational form than those which predominated when we were manufacturing steel, textiles, and relatively stable products, like the traditional automobile. For the last, American companies until recently had the luxury of undertaking slow-paced "planned obsolescence." Many of the new technologies and innovations require a structure and style of organization with much more emphasis on the individual.

At least in the United States, large organizations were never as stultifying to the individual as Charlie Chaplin's depictions in *Modern Times* would have one believe. There has been a good deal of room to maneuver although, regrettably, the maneuvers were frequently unrelated to creative or innovative endeavors or to greater effectiveness. For managers, the maneuvering took the form of political games and status striving; for workers it was various kinds of output restrictions and antimanagement fun and games.

Human freedom implies, at least to me, not only the opportunity to realize individual goals of personal growth and expression but also an identification with larger goals. The latter provides some of the sense of accomplishment and identification that human beings need to rationalize their efforts and energies. Our compassion for social interaction and common purpose leads us to desire work that allows for mutually responsive relations with others.

The technologies that appear to be emerging and will have high survival value in a competitive world economy call for more educated initiative and intervention and the willingness to adapt and even improvise—worker and managerial levels alike—the very characteristics in which we can excel and in which we take joy in excelling.

NEW WAYS OF ORGANIZING INDUSTRIAL WORK

WILLIAM FOOTE WHYTE

According to conventional wisdom, there are just two ways to organize industrial work: government ownership and control of the means of production, or private ownership and control.

We are now recognizing enough difficulties with both alternatives to provoke us to search for some other way. Even if government ownership would not result in an economy like the repressive totalitarianism of the Soviet Union—an unlikely outcome in the United States, given the great differences in our histories and cultures—government ownership would nevertheless present certain extremely difficult problems. Government ownership brings large, unwieldly bureaucracies, rigid in structure and ill-adapted to changing conditions. Also, particularly in developing countries, the tensions are manifest between the government-owned firm as an industrial enterprise and as a means of providing jobs for the inhabitants. One of the most difficult tasks in managing these enterprises is to avoid overloading the organization with more employees than are needed in order to raise the job rate.

In many cases, private enterprise presents a welcome contrast to the deficiencies we find under government ownership and control. In the United States as well as elsewhere there are many highly successful and socially responsible corporations. Nevertheless, the loss of U.S. market dominance has unleashed a profound doubt about the virtues of U.S. management techniques and even of the private enterprise economy. It was as late as 1968 that the French journalist Jean-Jacques Servan Schreiber published his best-selling *American Challenge,* in which he claimed that U.S. managers were so much more efficient than European managers that American interests were taking over the Continental economy.

No one talks that way any more. Americans now encounter frequent criticisms for being so narrowly focused on making money that we neglect the needs of society and of our own organizations to produce high-quality goods at low cost. We even hear business leaders unashamedly say that it is cheaper to buy a company than to build one. The game of taking over other companies, or avoiding being taken over, has led to increasing the ascendancy of lawyers and financial specialists to the top policy-making positions. Furthermore, at the same time that we hear claims that only private companies can create jobs and fill the nation's needs for employment, it is becoming increasingly evident that our largest and most prestigious corporations contribute little or nothing to the net increase in jobs. As they substitute capital for labor, they are eliminating jobs about as fast as they create them.

Is there another option? Suppose workers owned or controlled their companies? I am not suggesting a complete transformation of our economy into one based on worker ownership, but I argue that there is sufficient promise in such unfamiliar organizational forms to warrant our interest. Perhaps in our role as citizens, we should encourage this kind of social experimentation.

In the nineteenth century, leaders of the Knights of Labor took a strong interest in worker cooperatives, but the American Federation of Labor and the advocates of collective bargaining won the ideological argument, and worker ownership was relegated to the fringes of labor's concerns. In early twentieth-century England, it was Beatrice and Sidney Webb who laid down a negative judgment on the prospects for this form of industrial organization. Since the Webbs were well known not only as social scientists but also as friends of labor, their views had great weight among activists and social theorists.

Although some recent critics of their thesis have argued that their interpretation was unduly pessimistic, the nature of the Webb case nevertheless warrants serious attention even today. They found that worker cooperatives tend to suffer from a chronic shortage of capital. The workers are dependent on private banks for loans, and bankers are unsympathetic to this form of organization.

Worker cooperatives tend to be technologically stagnant. Even when they begin with state-of-the-art technology, worker-owners are inclined to prefer immediate financial rewards over long-run gains. Therefore, the cooperatives fail to modernize their technology, and eventually they are left behind in the competition with private firms.

Finally, there is the phenomenon that I call *collective selfishness*: they cease to exist as cooperatives either because they fail financially and go out of business or because they succeed. In the latter case, with the passage of time and the expansion of the firm, the original owners realize they will dilute their own equity if they admit new workers to ownership. New workers instead become hired labor, thus creating a two-class system within the firm. When the original members reach retirement age, they are naturally eager to sell their shares in the company, but by then the value of the stock in a successful firm has risen beyond the reach of the non-owner workers. Therefore, the shares of stock that control the company slip away from the workers.

These are real problems, but are they inherent in worker ownership? Not necessarily. In the United States, beginning in the 1970s, the need to save jobs inspired employees to take over a number of plants threatened with shutdown. In the same period, partly in response to legislation supporting employee ownership, a rapidly growing number of firms started out with at least partial employee ownership, and other firms converted to this form without the threat of shutdowns.

The emergence of employee-owned firms out of threatened plant shutdowns is dramatic and has received wide attention from the press. The publicity has created the false impression that employee-owned firms predominantly have this origin. In fact, according to Corey Rosen, director of the National Center for Employee Ownership, in 1983 only about 1 percent of the five to six thousand firms existing in the United States with a significant percentage of employee ownership were the result of an effort to save a plant or company from shutdown.

There are indeed a number of highly successful companies that have been in substantial measure employee owned from the outset. For example, W. R. Gore—makers of Gore Tex, the popular fabric coating—is 85 percent owned by employees, and the firm continues to expand and profit. Science Applications in California grew from three hundred to four thousand employees in the decade from 1972 to 1982, and the value of its stock went up one thousand times. Employees own 85 percent of that stock.

To be sure, none of the cases mentioned have been in existence long enough to render a final judgment about their long-run viability, but they and a host of others indicate that employee ownership is a rapidly growing phenomenon in this country.

Even though the cases of employee ownership arising out of conversion of private firms to save jobs constitute only a small minority in the total field, we estimate that within the last decade well over fifty thousand jobs have been saved by such conversions. Furthermore, through 1983, among the fifty to sixty cases of this type, we know of only four in which the converted firm subsequently failed, with those ultimately losing their jobs numbering less than one thousand. Since this record has been achieved under the most adverse conditions, this type of case is worthy of serious attention. Furthermore, such conversions have continued to occur in important companies in vital industries. The employee-owned company at Weirton, West Virginia, with close to eight thousand employee-owners, is currently the eighth largest steel company in the United States.

Conversions to employee ownership have occurred in two distinct periods of development, which fall neatly in two decades: the 1970s and the 1980s. In the 1970s cases, one or more members of local-plant management took the initiative in organizing a campaign for employee ownership, in order to save the plant. Surprised and pleased to discover that they might not lose their jobs after all, workers cooperated with local management but made no demands for control or participation in decision making. Local union leaders reacted similarly. Ambivalent and confused, higher-level union officials generally remained on the sidelines through the conversion process. They could hardly argue that unemployment was better than employee ownership, but neither could they figure out what the role of the union might be in an employee-owned company.

In one of the earliest cases, workers and local-union leaders at South Bend Lathe were persuaded to trade their pension plan for stock ownership—a decision bitterly fought and highly publicized by the national leadership of the United Steel Workers Union. The publicity surrounding this case gave union leaders the impression that conversion to employee ownership necessarily involved trading in a pension plan or making other major sacrifices. However, the South Bend Lathe case was an exception to the general pattern of the 1970s. In other conversions, little if any financial sacrifice was imposed on workers. In a number of these cases, the plant being shut down had been making a profit. The shutdown decision corresponded to top management's desire to move its capital out of marginally profitable plants into more lucrative areas. In other cases where the plant had been losing money, local managers attributed these losses to mismanagement by remote control from conglomerate headquarters. If the plant could be managed by people who knew what they were doing, profits could be won. Under such conditions, there was no need for workers to undergo major sacrifices.

In the early 1980s there was a sufficient shift in the nature of cases to warrant speaking of a new pattern. Largely in response to the financial distress of certain companies, local union leaders stepped forward to organize the campaign to save jobs through employee ownership. Furthermore, they sought to establish worker participation and at least a share of control.

Higher-level union leaders have come to recognize that, whether they like it or not, employee ownership is happening. The national offices of the unions must therefore be involved, at least to the extent of providing advice and information to local union officers and members.

For the emerging pattern of union initiative in employee buyouts, the landmark cases were Rath Packing Company and Hyatt-Clark Industries. Although in both cases the employee-owned firms eventually had to shut down, these firms received extensive media coverage and were intensively studied by behavioral scientists. The lessons to be drawn from these experiences therefore became of great interest to practitioners as well as to researchers. Those lessons can be summarized as follows:

(1) The Rath case demonstrated that it is possible to create a democratically controlled Employee Stock Ownership Plan (ESOP). Up until this time, it had been generally believed that the ESOP must be structured so that voting stock was allocated in terms of level of employee compensation, thus giving managers power far beyond their numbers. It was also assumed that all employees should have a right to sell stock allocated to them. If that were the case, and large numbers of workers preferred immediate cash to worker majority control, members of management could buy up enough additional stock to secure firm control of the company.

The Rath ESOP, designed by attorney Jack Curtis, provided for a radically different structure. The employees voted to accept a company, thus giving them 60 percent of the total shares outstanding. To keep this 60 percent share in a block, the union leaders set up a trust to vote the stock. The trustees were then elected by the employees on the basis of one employee, one vote. In other words, Rath plugged into the ESOP the basic democratic principle of worker cooperatives.

Before encountering the Rath case, leaders of the Industrial Cooperative Association (ICA) had been highly skeptical of ESOPs, regarding them as necessarily biased against workers. Recognizing the advantages of working within a framework having federal government support, ICA now began promoting democratically structured ESOPs with its own adaptation of the Rath formula.

(2) An employee buyout of a failing company is an uphill struggle at best and is unlikely to be successful unless it is supported by both a highly competent management and an effective program in worker participation in decision making. In the Rath case, with training and technical assistance from Brigham Young and Cornell Universities, the union leaders and production managers developed an effective joint program to improve shop-floor efficiency. Unfortunately, that program was not combined with a competent management. In fact, our follow-up studies found top management extremely disorganized, offering nothing remotely resembling a management team.

(3) When union and management have had a long history of conflict, success depends upon their ability to transform a power struggle into a jointly led cooperative and participative program. In the Hyatt-Clark case, intransigent union leaders confronted a chief executive officer determined to maintain management's traditional prerogatives. An incipient worker-participation program was aborted when the recently appointed CEO saw it as a union-led power play. When the parties faced bankruptcy, they finally sought to establish a basis for cooperation, but by then it was too late.

What may eventually turn out to be the most significant of all these cases for the long run arose in Philadelphia in 1982, when the Atlantic and Pacific Tea Company (A&P) announced its plans to close nearly all of its supermarkets in that area. Fortunately, a resourceful union leader, Wendell Young, president of Local No. 1357 of United Food and Commercial Workers Union, had anticipated the decision and had been thinking for some time about the possibility of employee ownership. Young and his union associates, with the technical assistance of consultants Sherman Kreiner and Andrew Lamas of Philadelphia Area Cooperative Enterprises (PACE) and of Jay and Merry Guben of Grey Areas, worked out a highly innovative contract with A&P. In return for pay and benefit concessions of somewhat more than 20 percent, A&P agreed to reopen most of the stores, at the same time making substantial investments in refurbishing them, as a newly organized subsidiary, Super Fresh Food Centers, Inc. In addition to getting the jobs back, the union secured an option to buy any store that A&P decided to shut down in the future.

Of most interest to us, the union also secured a set-aside fund based on 1 percent of the gross receipts of the Super Fresh stores. This set-aside is being divided into two parts, one providing productivity bonuses to the A&P employees and the other being turned over to the newly created O&O (owned and operated) Investment Fund to provide financing, technical assistance, education, and research for worker cooperatives.

The original plan was for more than one-third of this set-aside to go to the O&O Investment Fund, thus providing the fund with approximately $2 million over a three-year period. However, problems between Local No. 1357, representing the clerks, and Local No. 56, representing the meat cutters—whose leadership had no interest in worker ownership—and technical legal difficulties in the terminology of the contract with A&P, forced Wendell Young to agree to a revised plan in which all of the set-aside goes first to individual workers, who are being urged by their union leaders to contribute 15 percent of their bonus money to the O&O Investment

Fund. In addition, the fund has received foundation grants and government loan funds to support its development activities.

Spain has experienced a dynamic and constantly expanding system built on worker cooperatives. The Mondragón cooperative experience began in 1943 when an extraordinary Catholic priest, José Maria Arizmendiarrieta, who had come to that small industrial town in 1941 as an assistant parish priest, organized a school to provide the sons of blue-collar workers with training in industrial skills. Beginning with two years of instruction for twenty-four students, that program has now expanded to thousands of students studying from high school through university degree programs in business administration and engineering. In 1956, five members of the first class in the school got together with eighteen fellow members to found Ulgor, the first industrial production cooperative. By 1959, Don José Maria had persuaded his disciples to organize a cooperative bank, designed primarily to finance and support the further development of all the cooperatives. The bank quickly became the central institution in the developing cooperative complex, which now includes Eroski, a consumers' cooperative with hundreds of stores throughout the Basque region and more than half a million members. It also includes Langun-Aro, a cooperative organization that provides social security and health care to the members and their families. Ikerlan, the industrial research cooperative, arose out of the educational system when it was still limited to high school and moved into a new building with substantial office and laboratory facilities in 1977.

Perhaps the most striking feature of Mondragón's success has been the ability of its leaders to create and sustain new industrial worker cooperatives. In the United States, various studies have indicated that, of all the businesses established in any one year, 80 percent will disappear by the end of the fifth year. In its early years, Mondragón experienced only one failure, a fishing cooperative, in one hundred tries.

Self-financing is a key to this extraordinary success. Profits are allocated in the following way: 10 percent to a community benefit fund, 20–50 percent to a reserve fund, and the remainder going to the worker members. However, instead of distributing member shares in cash, members agreed to allocate it to their accounts with the firm, adding each year their share of profits on top of their original contribution and the interest gained by these accounts. This money remains with the firm until the member retires or quits. The retention of the members' share in their accounts with the firm means that the firm effectively operates with a reserve fund based not just on funds set aside for that specific purpose but totaling approximately 90 percent of the accumulated profits. This extraordinary reserve arrangement not only helps to finance expansion in good times but also provides a cushion in periods when the cooperative experiences losses. The cooperative can dip into the capital belonging to the individual members to tide it over temporary downturns.

Another unique feature of the complex is its intricate set of intercooperative supporting institutions. Each cooperative is expected to manage its own affairs with full autonomy, but the support system provides assistance when needed. The key institution in this support system is the cooperative bank, the Caja Laboral Popular, which now has more than three hundred thousand individual depositors besides serving as the financial institution for all of the associated cooperatives. The Caja is not simply a bank. It has an entrepreneurial division with more than a hundred professionals working on research and development toward the creation of new cooperatives and providing emergency financial and technical assistance to save cooperatives running into serious financial problems. The worldwide recession of the early 1980s hit Spain particularly hard, with national unemployment rates topping 20 percent in some years, and unemployment in the Basque provinces was even higher. Up until then, the problem for researchers was to explain Mondragón's strong and continuing growth. By the 1980s, the research problem was to explain Mondragón's extraordinary ability to limit job losses and to reorganize so as to be able to renew growth. Member sacrifices and the emergency assistance of the intervention department of the entrepreneurial division of the Caja have been the principal keys to the survival and renewed growth of the cooperatives.

When a cooperative is in serious difficulty and calls for help, one or more members of the intervention department meet with the leaders of the cooperative and undertake a feasibility study to diagnose the problems and to determine whether and how the cooperative could regain its financial health. The plan mutually agreed upon between the Caja and the leaders of the cooperative in some cases calls for significant changes in the cooperative's management and may even include the temporary assignment of someone from the Caja as chief executive officer for a limited period. The reorganization plan also necessarily includes reductions in worker-members' pay, to replenish the reserve fund and the members' capital accounts and to pay back loans from the Caja. The reorganization plan is also likely to require some major changes in job assignments and even some reduction in the number of members of the given cooperative. However, all plans must be approved by majority vote of the cooperative's members, and the complex has elaborate arrangements to protect job security so that members transferred out of a given cooperative are assisted in joining a cooperative that is expanding and, for periods of temporary unemployment, receive 80 percent of their previous pay level.

The loan policies of the Caja are a major element in the support system, both for emergency interventions and for starting up new firms. The Caja regularly loans the member cooperatives money at 4 percent below national market rates, thus providing the cooperative firms with a significant advantage over private firms. Furthermore, if there is a prospect of long-run success but the cooperative is in a desperate financial position, the Caja provides loan money at zero interest for the first year, moving this rate up gradually over a five-year period until it reaches the 14 percent level.

Another way of looking at the complex is to note that it is designed to achieve vertical and horizontal integration without building large and rigid bureaucracies. The first firm, Ulgor, spun off new lines of activity as new cooperatives. Had this policy not been followed, Ulgor would have continued to grow substantially beyond its present size. As it is, the nature of the market and the interrelations among the products produced by Ulgor served to build a cooperative far larger than what the founders considered the ideal: up to 500 members. Ulgor in 1983 had 2,650 members.

Nevertheless, the founders managed to combine the economies of scale with substantial degrees of autonomy for the individual cooperatives by linking the spinoffs of Ulgor into a cooperative group called Ularco. To avoid putting the members of a spinoff cooperative at a disadvantage in earnings potential, the member firms of Ularco pooled profits and losses. Each firm handles its own manufacturing, engineering, and accounting but shares in personnel, finance, and legal services. The location of the personnel functions in Ularco makes it easier to transfer members temporarily from one cooperative to another to respond to declining market demand in one and expanding demand in another.

As Mondragón enters the 1990s, it is clear that the cooperative complex is building on a base of renewed strength and growth. The complex added five hundred jobs to its total employment in both 1986 and 1987. In 1988, with a growth in sales of nearly 15 percent, Mondragón added 1,050 jobs, bringing its total employment to over 21,000.

LEARNING FROM MONDRAGÓN

Although we can hardly expect to import the Mondragón model in its entirety to the United States, we can apply certain of its general principles. If we are thinking about securing long-run control in the hands of worker-owners, we must base control on labor, as is done in Mondragón, rather than on capital. The Mondragón formula for distributing profits to members by placing them in the accounts of the firm members rather than giving them out in cash also seems applicable anywhere, if the founding members can recognize the importance of building a strong capital base.

One general conclusion in the Mondragón case is clear: an individual, isolated cooperative in a sea of private enterprises has poor prospects for survival and growth. There is a great need to develop a supporting infrastructure.

In response to the growing interest in employee ownership, some elements of such an infrastructure are developing. The oldest and still-leading nonprofit organization, the Industrial Cooperative Association, provides technical assistance and credit through a revolving loan fund. Philadelphia Area Cooperative Enterprises (PACE) has also been developing these services, and credit unions here and there are showing interest in employee ownership. New York, Michigan, and Massachusetts have established state programs to provide services and credit, and other states are beginning to move in the same direction. By the mid-1980s, leading officials of some of the major American unions had committed their organizations to supporting employee ownership as a means of saving jobs.

Some of us in the universities have tried to respond, but our competence and resources are limited. For example, in the Rath Packing Company case, we were able to provide technical assistance in labor relations and quality of work life, to the extent of the funds we could raise, but Rath had urgent needs that we could not meet for the kind of technical assistance in business administration regularly provided by the intervention department of the Caja's entrepreneurial division. Furthermore, Rath fell victim to the rules of the banking game as practiced under private enterprise. A Mondragón cooperative in severe financial difficulty has the opportunity to secure new financing at substantially below market rates. In contrast, Rath had to pay a premium on its loans, further undermining its chances of regaining financial health.

Judging from the Mondragón experience, employee-owned firms have a wide variety of needs that can be met by no single type of assistance. They need low-interest loans, educational and research services, technical assistance in financial analysis, business administration, and labor relations, plus a means of integrating these supports especially in crisis periods when major changes must be carried out in a coordinated manner.

Mondragón's success depended in large measure upon the abilities of its leaders to create social inventions, arising out of their own culture but without previous organizational precedents. It remains to be seen whether we have the will and the creativity to invent those organizational arrangements, social policies, and programs necessary to build the employee ownership movement of the future.

LOOKING AHEAD

While interest in employee ownership and worker cooperatives continues to grow in the United States, in the 1990s growth is likely to come much more rapidly abroad. As economic policymakers and political leaders in the People's Republic of China, the Soviet Union, and Eastern European nations have come to recognize the inability of government ownership and control of the means of production to meet the needs of their people, they are desperately seeking different forms of economic organization.

"Privatization" has become a popular slogan in the United States and is even coming to be accepted in some quarters abroad, but how do you privatize government-owned firms in a country that has no large and affluent private firms and very few individuals with the massive resources needed to make the necessary investments? Employee ownership is coming to be recognized as one of the major ways of making the transition to a market economy.

If national policymakers move in this direction, they face enormous problems of choosing forms of employee ownership appropriate to their nations, working out supporting legislation and regulation, and providing the necessary financing and technical assistance to make for a successful transition. To solve those problems, policymakers are increasingly looking for guidance from abroad.

Early in the 1970s, when some of us got interested in action research on employee ownership and worker cooperatives, we found ourselves on the fringes of our national economies, with hardly any practitioners sharing our interests. By the late 1980s, that scene had dramatically changed. Now the problem is not a lack of practitioner interest in what we have learned but rather our own worries over whether we have learned enough to help practitioners to capitalize on the enormous opportunities and challenges they are suddenly facing.

In this international network of students and practitioners of employee ownership, several individuals and organizations are playing key roles. David Ellerman, economist of the ICA and a student of both ESOPs and Mondragón, has been on study and technical assistance tours to the People's Republic of China, the Soviet Union, and Poland. Norman Kurland, an attorney who worked with Louis Kelso, the creator of the ESOP idea, has established the Center for Economic and Social Justice to promote international study and action on employee ownership. In London, Robert Oakeshott, the man who introduced Mondragón to the English-speaking world, has created Job Ownership Ltd. as a vehicle to promote democratic forms of employee ownership at home and abroad.

In less than a generation, a field of ideas and information of interest to few academicians and far fewer practitioners is becoming a major supporting element for a worldwide social movement.

Author's note: those with a special interest in Mondragón are referred to William Foote Whyte and Kathleen King Whyte, *Making Mondragón: The Growth and Dynamics of the Worker Cooperative Complex* (Ithaca, N.Y.: ILR Press, 1988).

CONTRIBUTORS

GWENDOLEN M. CARTER, professor emeritus of political science, Indiana University. Major publications on Africa include *The Politics of Inequality: South Africa since 1948; Which Way Is South Africa Going?; African Independence: The First Twenty-Five Years; Continuity and Change in Southern Africa; Southern Africa: The Continuing Crisis* (2d ed.); and *International Politics in Southern Africa,* co-edited with Patrick O'Meara.

GORDON W. ENGDAHL, business consultant. Retired in 1983 as vice-president, human resources, 3M, after a forty-year career there.

ORVILLE L. FREEMAN, chairman of the board, Business International Corporation. Governor, State of Minnesota, 1955–61; U.S. Secretary of Agriculture, 1961–69. Publications include *World Without Hunger* and *The Multinational Corporation: Instrument for World Growth.* Serves as a director of Worldwatch Institute and the World Future Society. Chairman of the advisory committee of Hubert H. Humphrey Public Affairs Institute, University of Minnesota; chairman of the board of governors, United Nations Association of the USA.

CHARLES F. GALLAGHER, senior adviser for Spain and Portugal, Morgan Guaranty Trust Company; consulting associate, Universities Field Staff International. Published *The United States and North Africa; Hawaii and Its Gods: A Cultural History;* and *African One-Party States* (co-author).

ABBOTT GLEASON, chairman and professor, Department of History, Brown University. Author of *European and Muscovite, Young Russia;* co-editor, *Bolshevik Culture: Experiment and Order in the Russian Revolution.*

LADONNA HARRIS, founder and president of Americans for Indian Opportunity; human rights and political activist. Member of the Comanche Tribe.

A. E. DICK HOWARD, White Burkett Miller Professor of Law and Public Affairs, University of Virginia. Chairman, Virginia Commission on the Bicentennial of the U.S. Constitution. Publications include *The Road from Runnymede: Magna Carta and Constitutionalism in America* and *Commentaries on the Constitution of Virginia.*

JOSÉ ANTONIO JÁUREGUI, Oxford-educated Spanish anthropologist and author; taught at the University of Southern California, now residing in Spain. Books include *The Rules of the Game: The Tribes* and *The Rules of the Game: The Sexes.*

DAVID F. LINOWES, Harold Boeschenstein Professor of Political Economy and Public Policy, University of Illinois; founder and consulting senior partner, Leopold and Linowes, C.P.A.s. Author of *The Corporate Conscience: Personal Privacy in an Information Society;* editor, *Privatization: Toward More Effective Government—Report of the President's Commission on Privatization* (1988).

ROBERT S. PECK, attorney and author, specializing in constitutional law. Former director of American Bar Association's programs on the bicentennial of the U.S. Constitution. Wrote *We the People: The Constitution in American Life,* the award-winning PBS series and its companion volume; *Speaking & Writing Truth* and *Constitutional Rights and America's Future* (forthcoming); and edited *Understanding the Law* and *The Blessings of Liberty.*

The late ITHIEL DE SOLA POOL was Ruth and Arthur Sloan Professor of Political Science, Massachusetts Institute of Technology. Publications include *Contemporary Political Science, Handbook of Communication, The Social Impact of the Telephone, Symbols of Democracy,* and *Technologies of Freedom.*

LEONARD R. SAYLES, director of research, Center for Creative Leadership. Books include *The Local Union* (with G. Strauss); *Behavior of Industrical Work Groups: Managerial Behavior; The Measure of Management* (with E. Chapple); *Individualism and Big Business; Managing Large Systems* (with M. Chandler); *Leadership: Personnel* (with G. Strauss). Fellow, National Academy of Public Administration and American Anthropological Association.

TAD SZULC, foreign affairs commentator and author. Since 1973, frequent contributor on foreign affairs to major U.S. publications and before that, *New York Times* foreign and diplomatic correspondent. Author of *The Illusion of Peace* and other books. Editoral board member, *Foreign Policy Quarterly.*

WILLIAM FOOTE WHYTE, professor emeritus, School of Industrial and Labor Relations, Cornell University. Author of *Street Corner Society, Man and Organization,* and *Organizational Behavior,* among others.